What People Are Saying About Emily T. Wierenga and *God Who Became Bread*

God Who Became Bread is iridescent with insight and arresting in its compassionate yet direct gaze upon how our deepest hungers, individually and globally, can only be fulfilled in Christ. From fasting to feasting, this beautiful and brave book shows us how God's plentiful redemption is, indeed, enough. Take and eat, and take and read: Wierenga's exquisite writing feeds us—body, mind, and soul.

—Dr. Carolyn Weber
Professor, New College Franklin
Award-winning author of *Surprised by Oxford*, now a feature film

Emily Wierenga's story is not only about overcoming her own deep pain, which led her to almost starve herself to death, but also about how she used that pain to help others. It led her to travel beyond the comforts of her home in Canada to feed others in impoverished places in Africa and South Asia. She came to realize that God is not a stern and even angry Being but is a compassionate and relational God who loves her and the people He sends her to. Emily wants to see people not only be lifted out of poverty but also flourish spiritually. *God Who Became Bread* will take you deep into Emily's life and help you understand what motivates this hero of the faith and her amazing compassion for the poor and the church wherever it is found. Emily's journalistic skills are evident as you embark on this journey with her!

—Greg Musselman
Minister at Large, The Voice of the Martyrs Canada
Former cohost, *100 Huntley Street*

I am completely undone. *Undone* is the only word I can stir up that describes my response to Emily Wierenga's new book, *God Who Became Bread*. The symbolism she presents is stunning; the rich lessons she layers in every section make me ravenous for more. There are sections of this book that I read with great heaves of my chest and gulps between my tears. How can a woman write with such simplicity and yet such texture? I believe the greatest endorsement one can give to a book is to humbly declare, "I wish I had written that book." I can assure you, I wish I had written this book.

—Carol McLeod
Best-selling author, Bible teacher, podcaster, and blogger
www.carolmcleodministries.com

I've known Emily for a very long time, and I have witnessed how she has completely given herself over to the will of God. She is incomparable. This beautiful book is her passion, penned onto pages. *God Who Became Bread* is a must-read that will move you. It is a testament to the transformative power of faith, reminding us that in God's boundless love, our hunger—both physical and spiritual—can be satisfied, and through us, the hunger of the world can be met.

—Jennifer Dukes Lee
Best-selling author, *Growing Slow*, *It's All Under Control*, and *Stuff I'd Only Tell God*

So many of us go through life with a vague hunger for more. *God Who Became Bread* is an invitation to explore what will truly satisfy your soul—a feast of grace, hope, and resilience. Emily's words will help you settle deeper into your seat at the divine table, where you're fully known and loved, where you've always belonged.

—Holley Gerth
Wall Street Journal best-selling author of *What Your Mind Needs for Anxious Moments*

Emily Wierenga masterfully and tenderly feeds the hungry soul with life-giving stories of true feasting in the most unlikely places. Her pen becomes a paintbrush with sweeping strokes of grace that invite readers to pull up a chair to the table and listen in on intimate conversations of what it truly means to be full—to live full. Emily shows us how to not only feast on the Bread of Life, but also break bread and share the grace with others.

—**Sharon Jaynes**
International conference speaker
Best-selling author of 25 books, including *When You Don't Like Your Story: What If Your Worst Chapters Could Become Your Greatest Victories*

Emily Wierenga invites us on a tapestried journey of remembering what has long been forgotten—the blessing of bread, the rituals of being fed, the celebration of feasting. But she also invites us to remember and give weight to the hurts that have shaped us, the people on the other side of the world we too often ignore, and, perhaps most importantly, the God who weaves our hurts and our hearts into true healing. Read this book. Be filled. And remember.

—**Sheila Wray Gregoire**
Founder, Bare Marriage

Many of us have been starving for so long, we no longer feel the hunger in our souls. *God Who Became Bread* will awaken that hunger—and it will also satisfy it. This is more than a book; it is an intimate invitation to Christ's table, to feast with the *God Who Became Bread*. Wierenga's poetic, raw, achingly beautiful prose will take you to tables around the world and awaken your hunger for God in such a way that you will be changed, you will be filled, and you will want to feed others who are starving for His love, warmly inviting them, "Come to the table."

—**Rebekah Fox**
Blogger, BarrentoBeautiful.com

Emily Wierenga's memoir God Who Became Bread features stories of food, faith, family, and friendship from around the world. Emily encourages readers to experience God's grace and feast on the living Bread of Jesus Christ and the nourishment He offers, reminding us that, before His death, rather than performing additional miracles, Jesus prioritized sharing a meal with His friends: "Maybe eating together is a miracle." With lyrical prose and honest reflections on her complicated and sometimes life-threatening relationship with food, Emily explores how God sustains us through both the physical gift of food and the sacrificial blood of His Son, consumed yet never depleted.

—**Dawn Camp**
Author, *It All Began in a Garden*

Emily Wierenga has the soul of an artist and the heart of a missionary. Emily wrote this book because she was asked to, and not without first seeking God's heart to know if He would have her devote the time and energy necessary to tell the story well—a goal she far surpassed. Emily invites us to a feast. She sets a warm and welcoming table with her poetic words, feeds us the living Bread, and inspires us to go and serve others the feast we've freely received. I pray this book finds its way into the hands of many, and that they follow Emily's footsteps into the joy of becoming broken bread for the world.

—**Jeanne Damoff**
Author and speaker
Secretary, The Lulu Tree Foundation

Some years ago, Emily Wierenga put aside the platform she'd built as an author, set aside her ambition, and took up a calling to live the Word rather than simply write about it. Since then, the Lord has blessed countless people around the world because of her offering. It has been my honor and privilege to serve alongside Emily at The Lulu Tree, learning from her humble obedience and deep desire to please the Father above all else. I have never met a braver, stronger person than Emily. And yet her strength comes from the Spirit who fills her as she empties herself, loving the least of these with everything she has. As He often does, God returned Emily's sacrifice with compound interest. *God Who Became Bread* is a beautiful work of redemption, a powerful reminder that our God is a miracle worker, an abundant provider, and a tender and loving Father.

—**Erica Hale**
Vice President, The Lulu Tree Foundation

EMILY T. WIERENGA

GOD WHO BECAME BREAD

A True Story of
Starving, Feasting, and Feeding Others

WHITAKER
HOUSE

Cover photo courtesy of The Lulu Tree Foundation, 2022.

GOD WHO BECAME BREAD:
A True Story of Starving, Feasting, and Feeding Others

Emily T. Wierenga
emilytwierenga.com
thelulutree.com
emily@thelulutree.com

ISBN: 979-8-88769-225-8
eBook ISBN: 979-8-88769-226-5
Printed in the United States of America
© 2024 by Emily T. Wierenga

Whitaker House
1030 Hunt Valley Circle
New Kensington, PA 15068
www.whitakerhouse.com

LC record available at https://lccn.loc.gov/2024005159
LC ebook record available at https://lccn.loc.gov/2024005160

1 2 3 4 5 6 7 8 9 10 11 **ШJ** 31 30 29 28 27 26 25 24

Note to the Reader

Events in this book are described to the best of the author's recollection. Some literary license has been taken. Various names have been changed to protect people's privacy.

—The Publisher

"A 'companionable' person is someone who (etymologically at least) is willing to share bread with you. 'Companionable' is the adjective form of 'companion,' which ultimately derives from a combination of the Latin prefix *com-*, meaning 'with' or 'together,' and the noun *panis*, meaning 'bread, loaf, or food.'"[1]

To Jesus, my greatest Companion.
You are everything.

"Table Blessing"

To your table
you bid us come.
You have set the places,
you have poured the wine,
and there is always room,
you say,
for one more.

And so we come.
From the streets
and from the alleys
we come.

From the deserts
and from the hills
we come.

From the ravages of poverty
and from the palaces of privilege
we come.

Running,
limping,
carried,
we come.

We are bloodied with our wars,
we are wearied with our wounds,
we carry our dead within us,
and we reckon with their ghosts.

We hold the seeds of healing,
we dream of a new creation,
we know the things
that make for peace,
and we struggle
to give them wings.

And yet, to your table
we come.
Hungering for your bread,
we come;
thirsting for your wine,
we come;
singing your song
in every language,
speaking your name
in every tongue,
in conflict and in communion,
in discord and in desire
we come,
O God of Wisdom,
we come.[2]

Contents

PART THREE: THE FEEDING

PART FOUR: KOINONIA

Foreword

She quietly climbed the steps and took a seat at the back of the airport shuttle. Both the way that she moved and the seat that she chose communicated volumes about the woman I watched move past my second-row seat. We were on our way to the same writer's conference, and though I knew who Emily Wierenga was, having read her memoir *Atlas Girl*, Emily would not have known me had she looked up in my direction.

The very next day, Emily gave a short breakout session on the art of memoir writing. Seated again in the second row, I watched her intently as I listened to her share. More than gaining take-aways on the craft of writing, I left the class having learned a lesson about the craft of loving—loving God above all else. Emily was gifted as a writer and was there to help us hone our gifts for storytelling, but she was also gifted with a Jesus-hungry heart...and it whet my appetite for more of Him.

Hearing and seeing the way Emily's love for God overflowed into a generous love for others around the world cracked open my very small, myopic life.

We began our friendship that weekend, and since that time, I have moved up from the second row to get a front-row seat in Emily's life. Particularly, I've been privy to countless miracle-stories about what God has done through her humble, hungry life. It has been my joy to partner with Emily and The Lulu Tree ministry over many years, seeing the gospel message go out into the world through Bible-based mercy ministries.

In the pages of the book you are about to read, Emily shares multiple stories of the tables at which she has sat and the meals she has consumed (or denied herself) over the years. But one table-story strikes me most.

In the spring of 2018, I reached out to Emily and asked if there was some specific way that I could invite my online community of Jesus-loving friends to support the work God was calling her to in that season. Tearfully, she responded *yes* and then shared that their ministry partners in Uganda needed help hosting a "mama kit" outreach. I'd never heard of such a thing but was committed before she had finished her explanation. You see, the unsanitary conditions in which impoverished women in that country gave birth had led to a high rate of deaths among both mothers and babies. Pregnant women were required to bring their own sterile birthing kits with them to birthing centers. If they did not have the necessary supplies, they would not be allowed to receive medical help in childbirth.

God had led Emily and her ministry partners in Uganda to host a mama kit outreach in the villages. But they had no funds for mama kits. I proceeded to take the need to my online friends. Within a day, enough funds were raised for five hundred kits.

The day of the outreach, the sanitized, individually packaged birthing kits were piled high on a table of red African dirt. Ministry leaders from throughout the country gathered and prepared to distribute them, along with a simple meal and an extravagant serving of the gospel. However, the start of the outreach was delayed because pregnant women from near and far continued to come...and come and come and come.

The supplies that once had appeared so plentiful suddenly seemed like so few. Thankfully, the night before, Emily and her team had been led to pray that God would multiply them supernaturally. And right there on that miracle table, God performed a multiplying mystery like the fish and the loaves or the widow's oil. *Never, in all the handing out, did the mama kits run out. In fact, some were even left over. And a great many women came to faith that day.*

Knowing the author of this book has been a joy to me, but it is the wonder-working God she loves that is at the center of every story you will find within the pages ahead.

Pull up a chair at this literary table. It's time to feast!

—Wendy Speake
Author, *The 40-Day Feast, The 40-Day Sugar Fast,* and other
devotionals for Jesus-hungry women

Preface

*My longing will be the same in heaven as upon earth: to
love Jesus and to make Him loved.*
—St Thérèse of Lisieux[3]

Fellow pilgrim and God-seeker:

Have you ever hungered so much it hurt?

I did. I starved myself for four years and nearly died. I was
hungry for love and for Jesus and for everything to make sense.

Now I'm so full I can't help but feed others.

I don't have all the answers, but I know the One who does; and
in the coming pages, I hope to help you taste the God who became
bread and wine and life for you.

I've divided this story into four sections: "The Hunger," "The
Feast," "The Feeding," and "Koinonia." The section titles in the
first three parts represent elements of a feast: *table, bread, wine,
mangoes, fish, oil,* and *benediction.*

The final section, "Koinonia," is all about the ultimate feast, Communion—the Lord's Supper—and the depth of what this means for us ragged sinners saved by grace.

As we gather around the table, I pray that your appetite will be awakened, and that the more you partake, the more you will hunger for the only One who can truly fill. I pray you'll become glutted on God's goodness, then turn and feed this living Bread to a very hungry world.

Come with me to the table, friends. A meal awaits. Let's dig in.

Love, e.

Part One:

The Hunger

table

For all the tragic and ludicrous battles Christians have fought with each other for centuries over what actually takes place at the Mass, the Eucharist, Communion, or whatever they call it, they would all seem to agree that something extraordinary takes place. Even if the priest is a fraud, the bread a tasteless wafer, the wine not wine at all but temperance grape juice, the one who comes to this outlandish meal in faith may find there something to feed his deepest hunger, may feel stirring within himself a life even more precious, more urgent, more near than his own.
—Frederick Buechner, from *The Faces of Jesus*[4]

2023 – CANADA

Ours has holes and knots.

Two hundred years old, it's hewn from maple, with legs so short they're propped up by glass candle stems. At each end, it has

table 23

drawers packed with Bibles, a deck of playing cards, coffee coasters with cats on them.

It's circled by random chairs with stained beige cushions. Grooves of wood hold dry breadcrumbs.

We meet here three times a day. We laugh here, pray here, sometimes cry here. And always we eat here.

It's the table, the center of our home.

Even as it was the center of the early church.

Church was like home, back then.

And meals hold every home together.

I call my family for supper after trying to teach the boys how to place utensils as my British mum taught me—forks and knives tucked like straight arms next to the body (bowl), a spoon nuzzled next to the knife—but they just laugh and say, "Oh, Mom!"

Piano lessons and homework are half done; overdue library books litter the loveseat.

My husband, Trent, tosses his keys into the bowl by the fridge, takes his seat at the head of the table. There's a shoving-in of chairs and then, "Let's pray." Trent's voice leads us to a place of grace.

A young boy is with us this Wednesday. He and my older son will go to youth group afterward. I lift the silver lid of the stock pot and apologize. "I don't really know how to make soup." I'm always comparing my soup to my mother in law's, who is the finest cook I know. But after I dish out the bean broth and hand out thick slabs of bread with butter, my son's friend exclaims, "It's amazing!"—and I rest.

"So, how was your day?" I ask, and the kids' voices collide, filling me in on the who and what of their goings-on at school. Trent smiles at me over his bread and soup.

The broth is creamy, flecked with fresh parsley and dill, and plump with yellow beans from the garden, which sprawls sideways outside the front window.

Yet even as soup dribbles down my chin, and I reach for one of Mum's hand-sewn napkins, I remember: Years of hunger. Nights spent counting my ribs and listening to my stomach growl, a soothing assurance that I hadn't eaten enough to gain any weight and might even lose some. I remember sucking in my cheeks to make my cheekbones pop. I remember squinting my eyes to try to create laugh lines.

I remember doctors saying I would never be able to have kids because of the damage I'd done to my body, and I remember not caring.

Until I did care, that is.

Until all I wanted was life, my body feeling the pulse of a womb large enough to hold the world. A womb with no one to live in it.

"Mommy, I love you," my eight-year-old daughter says now, tucking her face into my arm like a bird in a nest, and I swallow. Her hair smells like wheat, like when you rub kernels together between your fingers.

"I love you too, hon," I say. The bread sticks in my throat.

Mum taught me how to make bread when I was young. Flour dust covering the counter and our skin, the air pillowing with the smell of yeast and dough rising. Then polishing the golden tops, hot from the oven, with butter. It was bread I didn't eat as a girl, but how I watched others eat it, pretending to taste every morsel, even feeling full afterward, Mum twisting her napkin in her hands, Dad reading the Bible a bit louder to all of us.

table 25

My daughter fingers the cloth napkin in my lap. "Grandma made these?" she asks. "That's pretty good."

I smile. "Yeah, Grandma was a good seamstress. She made a lot of my clothes when I was young because we didn't have much money."

My girl's head lowers, her pug nose wrinkling. "I miss Grandma," she says.

I pull her close. "I do, too, sweetie."

Trent grabs the Bible from the drawer. He's the first one done, as always. He learned to eat fast in the army. We're reading about David today, running from Saul, taking the holy bread from the temple, much like Jesus's disciples would take grain from the fields years later.[5] The temple and the fields, offering nourishment like a beaming woman, her apron dusted white.

I think of the song my pastor-father would sing to us as we lay in our beds on moonlit nights, his tenor a perfect pitch, a song based in part on Matthew 4:4: *"Man shall not live on bread alone, but on every word that comes from the mouth of God."*

"On every word...from the mouth of God."

And it tastes like the Eucharist.

Trent and I and the kids pray now; tonight, we pray for people whose names we've scrawled on paper. Names of those living on the streets, men and women we've met over the past year and given Bibles to, a fast-food gift card taped to the front. The kids argue because they all want to pray for Matthew, the man with the booming voice who thanked us repeatedly for the Christmas card we gave him. "It's the only card I've ever received!" he'd said, this man who grew up in residential schools. He told us about the priests and the beatings, but he still wore a crucifix around his neck.

After prayer there's a flurry of dishes and voices and me pulling out lunch boxes and the scraping of leftover food into pans for cats and chickens because nothing goes to waste here. It's something I was raised on, with the urgency of someone dying. To remember the poor and the hungry and to spare every mouthful. My parents were missionaries in the Congo and Nigeria. When you see people mix dirt with water to make a paste for their babies' bellies, you stop wasting food pretty fast.

Until I stopped finishing my meals for four years, that is, and Mum prayed harder for my soul.

I wipe the table clean now, think how tables suture my life together like stitches on a napkin....

There was the long, polished oak table at Auntie Gladys and Uncle Joe's farm. It was covered with a blue tablecloth, delicate chinaware, and a butter dish. Auntie Gladys and Uncle Joe were adopted relatives, no kids of their own. When my brother and sisters and I were children, they would "steal" us for sleepovers, take us on long snowmobile rides in the woods, and let us pick fruit from the orchard. Sometimes we'd do sing-songs in the living room, and Uncle Joe's eyes would twinkle as his bow danced like a tiny lady across the strings of his fiddle. How I wanted to feel tiny enough to dance. Later, we'd trek downstairs to the basement, where he'd show us his latest wood-carving inventions—model trains and all sorts of toys and creations—before we headed off to bed feeling so very loved, so very thought of. So very full.

There were the low-to-the-floor tables at the shabu-shabu restaurant, which was across the street from the apartment where Trent and I lived in South Korea. We'd sit with friends on cushions on the floor. The table had a hole in the center with an open flame, and a soup pot would be placed on top. We'd prong thinly sliced beef and vegetables, then stick them for minutes in boiling broth until they turned tender. We'd dip them in sauces, the meat and the vegetables tasting savory and sweet, and we'd swallow, do it all again. It was a Japanese hotpot dish, its name onomatopoeic, taken from the "swish, swish" or "shabu, shabu" sound the

table 27

ingredients make when stirred in the cooking pot. Once we'd finished the beef and the vegetables, we'd drink the broth itself. Cups of oolong tea between. Food was participation at the shabu-shabu table. It was ministry.

Then there were Africa's colorful plastic tables, which were the setting of many banquets. Food in Africa was a gift, often a sacrifice. Many goats and chickens were given to me, celebrating this awkward foreign lady entering the village. These people—some, at least—who had never tasted meat, now handing it over to me: a fowl or a goat representing school fees or medicine or charcoal they would now go without, gladly, with a laugh and a flash of bright African fabric. In Africa, honor is feeding the stranger. Honor is love.

And lastly I thought of the Communion table—one in particular, a makeshift table made sacred by God's presence there.

It was really just a stained leather trunk holding memorabilia from my childhood: cassette mixtapes of Bon Jovi and Bryan Adams, public speaking trophies, some melted candles, and old photos.

It was during the COVID-19 pandemic. We were homebound and desperate for fellowship, so I pulled out a loaf of homemade bread, and Trent filled a clay goblet with wine.

The quarantine had made us hungry for church, for the warm breath of others, for the shoulder-to-shoulder lifting of hands to God—together.

The day was white with winter. We draped the trunk with a lace cloth. It felt holy, somehow, like a marriage.

So our family became a church on the living-room floor. We formed a circle around the leather trunk, even as outside, snow fell thick. We were a mess of knobby knees and smelly socks, a messy people. A light flickered from the barnboard bookcase. A candle in the window flickered back, Morse code.

Trent opened the Bible and read about the Last Supper. Our three kids sat crisscross applesauce, tried not to play with the tablecloth.

Then Trent held up the slightly lopsided loaf, and I thought, "What a humble thing for Jesus to compare Himself to. Something so unceremonious, so plain, always paired with something else. Yet it fell from heaven."

We bowed our heads to thank Jesus for this offering, and we passed it to each other, tearing off pieces. Flesh for flesh. It tasted like mystery and flour.

Trent took the clay wine goblet, mountains painted on its sides, and we thought of Jesus's blood. What a generous and odd thing, this inviting people to drink your blood. His body a buffet. No wonder many of His followers left the day He said, "*Whoever eats my flesh and drinks my blood remains in me, and I in them.*"[6] Yet if they had seen how love poured from His pierced side, would they have stayed?

If only we knew the depths of His love, would we thirst?

There was the sipping and slurping and sharing of one cup, feeling very rebel-like, defying pandemic rules. My kids sat with purple mustaches, giggling and shushing each other.

And in the midst of our being very unsanctimonious, I heard a Voice.

Do this in remembrance of Me.[7]

It was the word *this* that crushed me.

All my life, *this* had been a sacred gesture. A religious symbol.

Now, however, *this* has become more.

It has become an invitation to feast with Christ at the table of suffering.

table 29

The Voice was quiet and unassuming. It could easily have been ignored.

I chose to listen.

Will you do this in remembrance of Me, Emily? Will you become broken bread and poured-out wine with no regard for your life?

Me, Lord? The girl who spat in Your face and punched holes into walls and ran from the church? Me? Broken bread?

There on the carpet, my kids and husband chatting, the candle and lightbulb flickering, Jesus looked at me, this God who became bread.

Much as He might have looked at Simon Peter that morning on the beach after His disciples had all but abandoned their Savior yet again.

Emily, do you love Me?

Yes, Lord, you know I love You.

Do you really love Me, Emily?

Yes, Lord.

Feed My sheep.[8]

bread

It's the really hungry who can smell fresh bread a mile away.
For those who know their need, God is immediate—not an
idea, not a theory, but life, food, air for the stifled spirit and
the beaten, despised, exploited body.
—Rowan Williams[9]

1987 – CANADA

Jesus tastes like macaroni and cheese.

Not like the dry brown bread served at Communion, all torn up into tiny pieces. No, Jesus tastes like Mum's macaroni and cheese because even though Mum uses powdered skim milk and margarine, macaroni and cheese tastes like love. And God is love.

At least that's what we are taught in homeschool and Sunday School, and the words "God is love" hang on our living room wall, stitched onto a large, rectangular piece of fabric.

I don't dare *say* that macaroni and cheese tastes like Jesus though. That's not something a good pastor's daughter should say. I just think it as I eat it, my short bowl-cut hair bobbing up and down as my fork rapidly meets my mouth, because love can't come fast enough.

Mum fills our plates high and slides green peas next to the cheesy noodles. They jostle together like they're trying to stay warm. Dad pours ketchup on his pasta until the cheddar cheese turns pink. I don't like ketchup, but Dad loves it so much that he even puts it on his eggs when we have special breakfasts. Most days, though, we eat homemade granola, our bowls dished up for us. The skim milk is often grainy and warm from being mixed that morning. It's made from powder, similar to what Dad used to package when he worked at a factory in Mitchell, Ontario—a job that paid for him to go to school to become a pastor.

Being in ministry means moving.

We've moved ten times since I was born. I'm seven now.

This year we moved into a giant, white-paneled house with a small white front porch and light blue stairs leading up to it. The stairs remind me of a blue tongue in a long, pale face. We live on Lucy Street in Richard's Landing, St. Joseph Island, Ontario. The land of puddingstone rock and great blue lakes.

On Sundays Dad sometimes wears a long, flowing robe, much like Jesus does in the movies, only Dad's robe has green sashes. He leads two services—one in Richard's Landing and another half an hour away in Hilton Beach. Thursday is sermon-writing day, when we don't dare glance at the white door of the study; every other day is choir practice, visiting church people, or going to Girl Guides and Boy Scouts. Saturday nights are bath nights, and Sunday nights are *The Wonderful World of Disney*. We pull the black-and-white television up from the basement, dust it off, and tweak the antenna until we can lose ourselves in its stories. Later we will have a color TV that sits on a stand in the living room, on top of one of Mum's crocheted doilies.

Sometimes, in the room I share with my two sisters, I lie in bed at night staring out the window. I look past the curtains Mum has sewn at the streetlights that blink like giant pupils in the dark. And I try to picture God.

I'm an artist. To me, the world is a combination of shapes and colors and faces—some happy, some angry, some beautiful, some not—with a background of crayon feelings, all of them swirling like a giant rainbow kaleidoscope. Despite all the old storybooks with their watercolor paintings of Jesus, I know that isn't what He looked like. Yet I can't picture Him either. I can't picture the most important face in my life, the face of the One who died for me. I have no photo of this God who became bread. All I have is unapproachable light.[10]

For a while, I stick a head on Him: I imagine a kindly old grandfather face, a face I can trust, with lots of smile lines and eyes that shine, and I try to curl up on His lap and talk to Him.

But then that begins to feel strange too, like I am making up God, and I'm not sure what is real anymore.

So, just in case God *is* real, I write out a list of names and pray them out, night after night, names and names of people. Because if God is real, then heaven and hell are also real, and I need to pray those people into heaven. Because they might not have anyone else to pray for them. So prayer becomes homework.

And I keep trying to see God, because macaroni and cheese only fills you up so long. And I am scared by how empty I feel at night, like someone has gutted out my chest, and it hurts to breathe.

Our feet were bare in that kitchen in Brazzaville, Congo.

Sometimes I sit on our floral couch and study the photo album Mum has meticulously labeled. I've heard stories about the events in the photos so often they feel very familiar.

In one picture I am standing on a wooden chair with an apron tied around my middle, blond hair crowning my head and the biggest smile on my face, like I was halfway through a laugh. My brother, wearing a diaper, is seated in a plastic bowl on the floor, his hands clinging to the chair. Mum stands beside me in a dress and a long white apron, thinner than I remember her, her mouth smiling but her eyes glassy with unshed tears. Mum didn't sleep well in Africa.

She is mixing something in a bowl, flour everywhere; no doubt it is bread because Mum was always making bread when she wasn't teaching us at the kitchen table or weeding her flower garden.

My parents were missionaries until just after I turned three. I didn't speak the whole time I was in Africa. I just watched. Dad taught agriculture to blind people, and Mum taught blind women how to crochet. Both were Jesus to people who couldn't see.

My brother was born in the Congo, six weeks premature. Dad had gone to tour agricultural work in another district, and Mum was alone with me when she went into labor. I guess a miracle happened because even though we were far from the nearest mission compound, with no car, the daughter of another missionary showed up that day with the mail. Mum told her what was wrong, and she brought the doctors.

My brother was born all jaundiced and angry-looking, maybe because he'd been woken up early, and he kept us up many nights after that, me gripping my Yogi Bear stuffie, missing the days when it was just Dad and Mum and me and our mango tree.

But soon my brother began to smile, and then he became my friend. We toddled around together on the red soil while Mum hung up laundry, and from my later trips to Africa, I imagine the trees around us were bursting with song through the colorful beaks of a dozen birds. The air no doubt smelled like coconuts and banana leaves.

Africa was full of shades and shapes and faces and tastes. Brown faces of women hanging their laundry from their green and yellow basins, singing their songs, their white teeth brimming with smiles and words I couldn't understand. Bright colors of dresses that swished on the mamas as they walked to the market, so fine, and the lemon yellow of the jerry cans they balanced on their heads as they walked. The shapes of the many kinds of vegetables and fruits that lay out in the sun to be purchased and brought home. Africa was mango juice dripping down my chin and fresh bananas from the trees and coconut, plump and white and milky. It was rice and peanut sauce and fresh pawpaw.

There's another photo of my brother strapped to Dad's back in the tilled-up earth of our Congolese garden, me crouched beside them, barefoot, like we're all planted and growing.

In Africa we were always barefoot, it seemed. Barefoot in the garden and in the kitchen. Barefoot in places where food grew and food was baked.

So it has always been easy, somehow, for me to associate the God who became bread with the God of Africa, the God of such vibrant faces and colors and shapes and tastes, for all of it was holy ground.

The ground in Canada is white with snow, and there are no bare feet. Snow covers the ground three feet deep, and we've made slides off the garage onto the snowbanks.

Every day, Mum sits my brother and me at the kitchen table for homeschool. We read our Bibles and pray, and we take out our textbooks, while our two little sisters scamper off to play dolls or do crafts. We study grammar and practice our handwriting and solve math equations. Later, Dad will teach us French and piano. In the afternoons, we sometimes learn about missions and the world, the needs of the many calling to us from the topographical face of the map.

And then it's playtime while Mum prepares supper or mends clothes or does laundry.

This particular afternoon, I'm playing dress-up with my brother and sisters. We're wearing old-fashioned clothes with pearls and suspenders and fancy hats and having the best of times. We're each other's only playmates.

Today a visitor has come to our home.

And somehow, from our imaginary land of fancy clothes and pearls, I hear her. The neighbor lady who's stopped by and is talking with Mum in the kitchen. She can see us laughing through the corridor that runs from the kitchen to the living room, and she asks Mum about us. Mum tells her our names and ages, pointing one by one, and when she points at me, the lady says, "My, she's a big girl, isn't she?"

It's the way she says it. "Big" sounds bad, like something monstrous. I suddenly feel very hot and stuffy and silly in my make-believe clothes and pearls. Not fancy at all.

And my stomach feels so very bloated. So very full of cheesy noodles, which no longer taste like love.

1989 – CANADA

I stop eating macaroni and cheese around the same time that Grandma Amelia dies.

Grandma Amelia is the next best thing I have to a close friend, because I have so few friends. She isn't really my grandma, either, but my grandparents live eight hours away, and we see them once a year, all dressed up and on our best behavior.

With Grandma Amelia, an elderly lady from Dad's congregation, I can sit cross-legged and eat cookies and drink tea and snort when I laugh and not worry about someone saying I'm not being ladylike or that I should be seen and not heard, because it's just me and her.

She teaches me to knit and to play Crazy Eights. And when she dies one day without warning, it guts me.

Dad is so busy with work and church, and Mum is so tired; I can't see God, and the one woman who was my friend left me without warning. And I can't get her back.

So, at nine years old, I stop eating.

All I can see for the next four years is myself.

I begin to stare for hours into the mirror at the image of the frightened little girl with the chubby cheeks and the bowl cut, and I begin to despise her because she seems very unlovable. And I think, if big is bad, then small is good, and maybe when I'm small, I will begin to feel the love I'm looking for.

I don't know anything about anorexia nervosa. We aren't even allowed to play with Barbie dolls or look at fashion magazines. Mum is concerned we'll become vain—or, worse, get an eating disorder—if we do.

But I get one anyway.

1991 – CANADA

It's suppertime, and the cuckoo clock on the kitchen wall tells us so. The wall is covered in flowered paper, and it has a chart tacked onto it now where Mum keeps track of what I've eaten and when I need to take a spoonful of cod-liver oil. It's her punishment for me when I don't eat enough, and it tastes like sin, but it's her way of taking care of her little girl because it's also chock-full of vitamins.

I'm eleven, and it's mac-and-cheese night again. But tonight I'm only eating a hunk of marble cheese. Two years earlier, when I began eating less of everything, it felt good to say no. The amount of food I ate became smaller and smaller until Mum started giving me the cod-liver oil, so then I switched to just one type of thing. It doesn't matter how much I eat of that one thing, but I've decided it can only be one thing. So Mum lets me have a chunk of cheese, and I gnaw at it with joy, taking little bites, savoring, while my family chews their noodles in silence.

I have a weight scale in my bathroom, and I rejoice when the digits get lower. I suck in my cheeks so I will look thinner. Mum and Dad begin sending me to school, hoping it will help. I make friends, but they are all slimmer than I am, so I feel huge and ugly and very much like a pastor's daughter. It doesn't help that I now have glasses and braces, complete with headgear. I write my essays and exams in such tiny letters that the teachers squint their eyes and complain. My bedroom is immaculate and my mood erratic.

"Emily, are you sure you don't want any noodles?" Mum asks again, her eyes big and blue.

I swallow, then erupt. "Mum! I've told you, I'm not hungry! Can't you just leave me alone?!"

Then I storm off to my room and slam the door, where I imagine Mum crying into her cloth napkin and Dad pulling out the Bible.

The next two years taste like hunger.

We have colorful afghans at home, crocheted by the blind women from Africa, and I wrap myself in them, trying to feel God's love around me.

And every night I watch the digits drop. I count each rib before I go to sleep, and I dream of food. Feasts, set before me. "*As when a hungry person dreams of eating but awakens hungry still.*"[11]

And I eat and eat and wake up, starving.

wine

We need to be aware of the importance of a ministry of absence.
This is very central in the Eucharist. What do we do there? We
eat bread, but not enough to take our hunger away; we drink wine,
but not enough to take our thirst away; we read from a book, but
not enough to take our ignorance away. Around these "poor signs"
we come together and celebrate. What then do we celebrate? The
simple signs, which cannot satisfy all our desires, speak first of all of
God's absence. He has not yet returned; we are still on the road, still
waiting, still hoping, still expecting, still longing. We gather around
the table with bread, wine, and a book to remind each other of the
promise we have received and so to encourage each other to keep
waiting in expectation for his return. But even as we affirm his
absence we realize that he already is with us.
—Henri Nouwen[12]

1988 – CANADA

There's a wharf by our church, smelling of fish and salted fries,
and a boardwalk that hugs it with long wooden arms.

And there's the place we never enter that holds a dozen bellies and a dozen songs not sung in church, and a dozen glasses filled with beer, as frothy as the waves that pound the shore. They call the wharf restaurant Whisky Rocks.

Down the street from the marina, just a stone's throw away, is the redbrick face of the United Church. Every Sunday after the ten o'clock service, Dad stands outside in his white robe, shaking people's hands. The congregation puddles onto the steps in dress slacks and nylons; they trickle down, pause to have their hands held by the minister, to answer his questions, then pour into their cars and meander on to lunch—tea, no doubt, and some polite sandwiches on white or brown bread (or, if they're daring, rye). The same triangle sandwiches that appear at a potluck, stuffed with egg salad or tuna salad or some other kind of salad.

Back inside the church, my parents dust the music sheets, stuff them back into the pump organ for another Sunday, slide the hymnals into the pews, and straighten the tithe envelopes.

I'm eight, and I wait, in my mushroom-style haircut and hand-sewn dress, with the rest of my siblings at the back of the church. Mum has tired eyes, but she patiently putters. Today we had Communion. And even as Mum packs away the tiny cubes of brown bread and the juice, and my brother says he's hungry, and my sisters chime in, I wonder why we aren't full. Why do we hunger more for our own supper than for the Lord's Supper?

Shouldn't Communion be the grandest of feasts, the one always on our minds, the one demanding every taste bud? To me, food is such a temporary thing, at best—a good taste, yes, but then it goes through the body; it creates energy, yes, but then we tire again.

Yet the idea of a Supper in which we consume Christ Himself, His body, His blood—a supper that promises we will never hunger or thirst again—this both interests and confuses me.

"*If you knew…who it is that asks you for a drink, you would have asked him and he would have given you living water,*"[13] Jesus says to the woman at the well.

Do we know Him?

Later the disciples return with food, and He tells them He has food they don't know about. They think someone has brought Him lunch. Food to them is something they can see.

The Samaritan woman gets it. She leaves her water jug, runs with the rivers inside of her.[14]

Mum finishes packing away the Communion cubes. The songs call from the wharf, and I wonder why we aren't allowed to enter such a happy place. And why church isn't a happy place, and why I want fish and salted fries more than I want God's body.

"Emily, your father is finished; let's go," Mum says, because I've been staring off as I do when I'm thinking hard.

One of the last things Jesus did on earth was to eat fish with His disciples in His new flesh-and-blood body. The resurrected Christ took time to eat. The God who made the fish, ate the fish.

His everlasting skin still bearing nail holes.

It's as if the act of eating is significant in itself. In spite of the food passing through us.

After eating supper, Jesus opened His disciples' minds, sealed shut for so long as if by rusty hinges, and filled them with knowledge of the Scriptures.[15]

Another opening of minds for knowledge happened after Jesus's walk to Emmaus with two of His followers. At supper, when Jesus broke bread—was it crusty and golden like Mum's?—scales fell from their spiritual eyes.

They ate, and they saw.

As if food is somehow necessary for seeing God.

After locking up the empty belly of the church, we climb into our old Plymouth Voyager. At the same time, the marina belches forth men who pat each other on the back, then head to their trucks.

"Buckle up, children," Dad calls from the front seat. He's removed the white robe and looks much like our father again.

We wash out the little Communion cups at home. They have tapered tops and a little ridge at the base that locks them into their wooden trays. They remind me of girls all dressed up, waiting for a dance. Dad puts them away for another Communion Sunday. Once every few months, he'll pull them out and take them to church and fill them with grape juice. It's a long time to wait.

My spirit aches for the tiny chalices that have been promised wine—the "*foaming blood of the grape.*"[16] Yet somehow we're convinced even Jesus drank grape juice. The fruit of the vine at the wedding of Cana must have been unfermented, some church people say. The jovial dancing and the laughter and the songs—just things of the Spirit, they say.

Yet Jesus was accused of being a drunkard.[17]

Some people smack their lips loud, swallow grace whole; others nibble it quietly, afraid to make a sound.

We are the kind who nibble it quietly, I think.

David tasted grace the day he was emptied of everything: his best friend, his home, his family. He ran to the temple because he was starving—not just for food but for love, for acceptance, for purpose. He ran, and he fed on the Bread of the Face, or the Bread of the Presence, still warm although it had sat out for a week. And God filled David's belly with Himself.[18]

Mum will turn the leftover Communion bread into bread pudding. When does the bread stop being holy? Or will it be holy pudding? The ark of the covenant was made of acacia wood and gold, but when Uzzah touched it, it became something more. Something dangerous.[19]

It's like the many people who pressed in to touch Jesus, but He only noticed the one. "*Who touched me?*"[20] He asked, because His robe had become something more in her hands. Something powerful that destroyed everything wrong in her body.

Communion can kill you. And yet we play with the cups.

Mum wipes down the blue-and-white tablecloth, and we eat tomato soup and grilled cheese sandwiches for lunch. Dad asks us what we learned in Sunday school. My youngest sister puts slices of marble cheese in her soup, and we make fun of her. She smiles with tomato-soup lips.

"Alright, Quiet Time," Mum says, stacking up the ceramic bowls. As she puts on the kettle, we climb the carpeted stairs to our rooms, get into bed. Sunday means Sabbath, means rest.

I lie there while my sisters quietly play with their dolls. I wonder what the grain tasted like, the tips of wheat the disciples snapped off on the Sabbath. Did they taste like grace? Does grace taste like a saltine cracker? Or like fish and fries?

I stare out the window at the tops of the sugar maples in our yard, their leafy heads like green afros. How would David ever get into our church since it was usually locked? Shouldn't God's house be open day and night, and shouldn't we be running to church, so hungry for God's presence?

My stomach rumbles.

I turn on my side, feel the slope of my jutted hip bone. I'm like an empty, songless bottle.

Sometimes we have potlucks in the basement of our church under flickering fluorescent lights. There are wiggly gelatin salads and casseroles and watery juice and triangle sandwiches with their crusts cut off. There are stacks of paper napkins and porcelain plates. There's the damp basement smell mixed with women's perfume.

Dad's tenor starts us off with grace, and we sing in rounds, "For health and strength and daily food, we praise Thy Name, O Lord."[21] The men sing first, then the women join in, their voices bowing and curtseying to each other.

And God's silhouette appears. Over the fold-out tables and the small-town chatter and the children giggling, God appears. In the awkward laughter and the mothers hushing crying babies, in the men adjusting their belts to make room for cake, in the women laughing as they begin to wash dishes, I see Him: the faint outlines of the Great I Am.

Then Dad and Mum lock up the church, and we say our polite goodbyes and walk home to our manse on Lucy Street, stuffed with gelatin and casserole and carrying with us the fellowship of food.

A few months later I get baptized.

Mum curls my hair with the curling iron, and I put on my nicest dress. I practice my smile in the mirror. I smooth down the ruffles on my sleeves and hope Dad is proud of me.

God and Dad are very similar to me, and sometimes I get them mixed up.

But everything at the baptism feels wrong, even though I answer the questions correctly:

"Do you believe Jesus Christ is the Son of God?"

"Yes."

"Do you believe He died for our sins, was buried, and rose again on the third day?"

"Yes." I say the word carefully, knowing the weight it carries.

"Are you committed to living for Him the rest of your life?"

"Yes...."

I'm reaching for the hem of His robe. But all I feel are a few droplets of water. They drip down my face like tears. Dad says words and puts his hand on me and prays. The congregation claps, and I'm handed a baptism plaque that already has my name on it. Like my answers didn't matter at all.

The plaque saying that I've been baptized, signed by my father, is like the scroll in *The Pilgrim's Progress* that was meant to give spiritual assurance to Pilgrim. Later, it will sit on the windowsill in my room, precisely in the middle, and I'll dust it every Saturday.

And when I stop eating a year later, I'll start to have dreams about food. And I'll wake up crying in the middle of the night and see the plaque, shadowed by night. So permanent and dark.

All I want is light.

These are the wilderness years. The years of the tiny honey wafers that fall from the sky and melt in the sun.

Canaan is a promise away—this land flowing with milk and honey. Honey is so expensive we can only slip a teaspoon of it into our tea. Cow milk is never served, only our usual powdered kind.

What a lavish waste, that land flowing with milk and honey. Like the pouring out of Mary's perfume.[22]

Surely the God who made something from nothing never lacked anything, ever. Yet He ate grain from a field on the Sabbath.

As if it wasn't about the grain.

As if it were more about the man whose hand had been crippled,[23] who likely laughed and broke the pious silence.

As if it were more about the juice turning to wine, and the handshake becoming a slap on the back, and the organ hymns becoming songs belted from full bellies.

2004 – CANADA

The wine bottle is empty now.

I'm twenty-four, newly married, and lying on a couch. Trent has gone to bed, and I can't sleep again because I'm not eating again, because I still mix up God with my dad. With the man who helped me with my math homework and who sang away the shadows and who sat like a general outside my room until I fell asleep.

Now I'm alone in the shadows. And the wine is real now—it's the "*foaming blood of the grape,*" but it's not holy.

I'm lying on a burgundy second-hand couch, and over my head, on the wall, is a long stretch of canvas upon which I've painted Jesus and the cross in thick acrylics.

The cross stretches against a backdrop of crimson. A tree rises from the bottom of the canvas, intersects the wooden beams of the cross that Jesus shoulders. A teardrop slips down His face. He stares down from the wooden beams of history into the eyes of

Eve, the original mother, who holds in her hands the seeds of sin—
an apple, to represent the fruit. And Eve is crying.

Jesus sees her. He weeps with her. He doesn't turn away.

Their sorrow falls on me, there on the thrift-store couch.

It's like a baptism.

mangoes

I think that the heart is a lot like those wonderful fruit, like coconut and mangoes, you know, you have to break the skin, you have to break it open to get to the good part.
—Saul Williams[24]

2014 – UGANDA/RWANDA

There are shadows here in Uganda, too, with a thin dress in them, and a thinner body, in the corner of a place that's supposed to be a hospital.

The only hospital in Kampala has no clean water. And right beside it, like an omen, sits the mortuary.

I smell urine and sweat and jasmine flowers baking in the sun.

People are laid out in beds, covered in white sheets like antique furniture. Other people—relatives who are waiting—lie below them on cold cement.

Everything here waits, like the unsteady feet of a bird on a wire between life and death.

At the age of thirty-four, I'm here in Kampala as one of a team of writers on a weeklong trip. We're bloggers sent by a nonprofit to write about what we see: three days in Uganda, two in Rwanda, and two in the air. I wear a Canadian hat and a pink scarf. I look like a tourist.

It's my first time back to Africa since I turned three. My home here is an air-conditioned hotel; my food, a buffet of kings, a spread from all nations. Outside, the poor lie at our feet like the beggar Lazarus.[25] Their houses are aluminum shacks. The sun glints off the roofs like someone signaling. Like a child with an empty tin can, aiming it at the light, saying, "Here I am. Help me."

So we write about the shacks, about the red and yellow flowers whose names we don't know but which look like hope to us. We write about the mango trees whose fruit is green skin stuffed with orange flesh. And we eat our buffet, and we wear our fuzzy slippers.

I see her now, in the thin dress in the shadows. Her lips play with a smile as she holds a tiny package. I move closer. The package is a baby who doesn't move. He's small, like a newborn.

"Congratulations," I whisper, because this antique furniture shop is quiet.

She looks at me. Her eyes are like wax candles, like she's been staring into glory. When she smiles, her cheekbones cut her skin like sharp knives.

I peek inside the blanket in her arms. Her baby's face is scrunched shut, eyes closed, faint gasps from his mouth, like someone stepped on a puffball.

He's the size of a womb.

My insides are carved out like sliced fruit. One year ago, my math-teacher husband, a rational man from a Calvinist church, had a vision of a baby girl. We had two tumbling boys at the time and fostered two other boys. Ours was a house of toy trains and building blocks and *Bob the Builder* and blue jeans.

The stick turned pink the day God spoke. He told me of a little girl He had planned for us. He told me I was pregnant now, and I assumed they were one and the same.

Until the cramping started. I was at a writer's conference. I texted Trent, "Babes, please pray. Something's wrong."

Then, the blood.

And the silence from God, what felt like four hundred years, even as we grappled with visions and words from above. Month after month, my womb stayed empty.

Finally, this blogger's trip—an invitation for the same month in which my daughter would have been born. I couldn't have gone if she had come, and so here I am, celebrating another woman's baby.

She must have just had him. She must be waiting for her husband to pick them up to go home.

"How old is he?" I ask. One mother to another.

Her feet shift. Her toenails are broken.

"Eighteen months," she says.

I clutch her arm like she can keep me from falling. The baby stays still. Faint puffs of air.

"I'm sorry?" I ask.

She swallows.

"He's one-and-a-half years old."

She looks at me, I at her. Two women. One baby. One God. A thousand questions.

This baby is maybe four pounds.

He should be crawling, walking, running, cheeks chubby as he tumbles and moves and gurgles and laughs and plays with sounds. He should be twenty-four pounds; he should be more than a wrapped-up body of tiny sighs.

His eyes stay shut.

Mine fill.

"Don't cry!" his mother says, her voice soft. "Don't cry. God is still alive."

I choke on her words, so beautiful and holy for such an awful moment. Her baby is dying, but God is still alive, and her faith slams hard into my soul. I'm revolted and reverent.

"Yes," I whisper. "God is still alive."

It's the raspy voice of Job:

"*Naked I came from my mother's womb….*"

The open place. The stripping-down-from-the waist-in-the-doctor's-office place. The place without walls.

"*And naked I will depart.*"

The arriving and the leaving in total need.

"*The* LORD *gave and the* LORD *has taken away; may the name of the* LORD *be praised.*"[26]

This baby is dying. But He lives.

Her eyes shine with the flicker of a whispered hallelujah.

This mother who's so thin she's also dying. No milk in her, no money to purchase formula, she and this baby drink weak tea.

"*This is My body which is broken for you.*"[27]

They starve because they have no food.

I starved although I had food. How dare I.

Yet she feeds me. At this table of suffering.

Night finds me on my knees in prayer for the pain of it all, for the many flightless birds, for all the mothers whose children starve.

And even as I bow, I feel her arms.

Mum's.

I'm eleven and trying to fall asleep when Mum comes in, lies down beside me, wraps her arms around me. She smells like flour dust and hand lotion. I stay still. Quiet. She must think I'm already sleeping.

I haven't let Mum hug me in two years. If I let Mum hug me, I might eat again. And if I eat, I might feel again. The pain of the world, the suffering I can do nothing about, the hurt when people or God disappoint me. It is safer to have walls, I decide. Walls built by exercise and scale-watching and calorie-counting. Walls that build a prison.

I hope she never lets go.

This woman in Uganda has no walls. She lives in the open, and she sees God. The One who, with one breath, could fix it all.

There's the sound of the air conditioner, the snores of my colleague, and the tap tap of Jesus on my shoulder.

"Let Me feed you," He says.

Africa, a breadbasket for my soul.

In my dreams I'm in the Congo, chasing iguanas and lizards across dusty dirt. The trees are large, their leaves the wide-open arms of a mother. Colors are everywhere, as if the earth has exploded in paint. Bright splotches on the beaks of the birds and the flowers on the bushes and the skirts of the women as they wash and sing and walk to get water.

When I wake it's as though I'm still asleep, my dreams lingering all around me. We walk the pathways of Katwe slum, marked by bare feet, bottles, and sewage.

Later I'll learn of the eggs that burrow into feet there. Of the jiggers that dig into soles.

I touch the skin of the people I'm passing, like a Jewish person touching a mezuzah, a parchment scroll inscribed with Scripture and affixed to a doorframe. These people are a mezuzah to me, the God who dwells in doorways. They are family—cousins, aunties, grandmothers. I shake the hands of as many as I can. Children's fingers are brown butterflies on my skin. I walk, their fingers flutter, and we giggle.

Around a corner there's a tiny girl in a dirty skirt and pink shirt. She barrels toward me like she knows me. Falls into me, wraps her tiny arms around me, and we stay there in the middle of that hug for a long time.

It's like my daughter has finally found me.

We fly now, low, in a bush plane over northern Uganda, over thatched roofs and people's lives. The sky holds us like a blue parachute. I see charcoal fires and round clay huts with yellow grass stuffed in cracks. These homes are small and flammable, and nothing but the eye of God would miss them if they burned down.

The same eye that witnessed the wrath of Joseph Kony, a former altar boy who never finished elementary school, who lit up a host of villages in the 1990s, who abducted over sixty thousand children: the boys, forced to murder their families; the girls, to give birth to soldiers' babies.

We've come now to meet these children. They've stretched, like flowers, into men and women, trained in welding and tailoring by the nonprofit we're writing for. The women stand in garden rows, infants growing from their hips.

They glance down as we pass. We grip each hand. Some of the babies whimper. I'm like a ghost with my white skin. I stare at the beauty of each baby, born from hate. They look like redemption in diapers.

Later we enter the tailoring school. The girls show us their work. I hug them before I leave, the rest of the team waiting, patient. As I make my way to each girl, tears pool in my eyes. "I love you," I say. They look up, and they see me.

And they smile.

Rwanda is next, with its clean streets. "Just because we're poor doesn't mean we need to be dirty," the country's president has said. A stray plastic bag cannot be found. The roads are immaculate, swept raw with grass brooms. As if Time is scrubbing away the genocide with a bucket of hot water.

But when the ground dries, it's still red.

We've flown into Kigali, and now we're in a bus headed to the villages. Boys jump on the tailgate for a ride.

It's the land of a thousand hills. The horizon is green with trees, like tall men dancing. When we stop and exit, a cloud of kids gathers. They put hands to lips; say, "Water, water"; do the puppy-dog look my kids do back home. Most of them are half-dressed, without shoes. We're here in Widow's Village, a place created by the 1994 genocide, a place filled with women and children who lost husbands and fathers in the war.

When no one's looking, I give the children water. I grab a box of plastic bottles from the bus, hand them to the kids, and—for a minute—I feel good. But there isn't enough water to go around, and soon the fighting starts, the bottles are emptied, and the ground is a mess of crushed plastic. An older kid smiles, says, "Give me money."

I'm like Moses when he hit the rock.[28]

I sit, sad, among the women on the ground in my long, dusty skirt. The widows put their arms around me, their faces like dry brown leaves.

A child crawls into my lap. Her head is shaved because of the lice, her skin soft and warm. She smells of eucalyptus.

A woman wrapped in a scarf and a skirt, wearing a worn Coca-Cola T-shirt, rises beside me. She's Tutsi. She speaks in Kinyarwanda, and her words are translated for us. It's a pulsing story of loss. Her husband and sons were all murdered in the war by extremist Hutus, all within hours of one another. Her daughters, gone mad with grief, left their children with her, and she is now caring for them. She smiles, the parting of her lips like the splitting of a dried apple's skin.

"God is good," she declares in English, as though she doesn't want this truth lost in translation. And she sits.

When I was fourteen, wearing bell-bottoms and listening to Bon Jovi, over eight hundred thousand Rwandans died.

The woman turns to me then. She touches my arm. "God is good," she says again.

Somewhere an osprey sings. It sounds like a kettle starting to boil.

At the Genocide Memorial, I break like brittle bones. They ask us to smile for a group photo. I can't.

We're just outside the visitor's center, and I'm steps away from the graves of two hundred and fifty thousand murdered victims.

A wall of names records nearly one million victims killed in just ninety days. The wall hedges trees known as the Forest of Memory.

The atmosphere of the memorial is quiet with the heavy breath of death. A tall Rwandan in sunglasses tells us the memorial is free to the public because they want people to remember.

The center opened in 2004, the year after Trent and I got married.

Inside the building, I see photos and artifacts—memories and remnants of cuisine and arts and people.

And then I read about the extreme members of the Hutu tribe, how they determined to exterminate the Tutsis, even as moderate Hutus tried to protect them—how it wasn't just about killing off an entire people group but about causing them to experience an excruciating death.

The hallway curves into a room filled with the skulls of children, placed tenderly beside little shoes, a crucifix. There's a life-sized photo of the child whom the skull belonged to, a record of their last words, intimate details about their favorite things.

My spirit heaves. I stumble along the hallway, out of the building into the scorching heat of noon. The air smells like *mandazi*, a sweet fried dough. I find a bench.

It's as if Hope has miscarried.

It's as if the worst possibility of man is on display in this museum: four hundred thousand children murdered by machetes.

There is so much room for evil in the human spirit. And that potential swallows me.

I cry, and I'm afraid: for myself, for my children, for my neighbor. I'm afraid of our sinfulness.

An African priest passes me, eyes lowered, shaking his head. He says something like, "Appalling, appalling."

I look up.

I'm in a garden. Roses, everywhere.

Then I see it: a rose at my feet. It's broken, yet somehow it blooms.

Torn from its life source, yet its petals sing a scarlet aria. They sing of the fifth verse of Psalm 23: "*Thou preparest a table before me in the presence of mine enemies.*"[29]

And God speaks.

If there's that much room for evil, daughter, then there's that much room for good.

fish

I was nothing but a body. Perhaps less than that even:
a famished stomach. The stomach alone was measuring time.
—Elie Wiesel[30]

1993 – CANADA

My body is my gospel.

I count my ribs like a Catholic girl counts her rosary beads. One by one, I touch them as I lie there in the dark. Only I don't say, "Blessed art thou among women…." Instead, I chant a list of what I've eaten that day. It's a short mantra.

The hungrier I am, the holier I feel.

I'm thirteen now. I share a birthday with Elvis Presley. My friends have their periods. Their bodies have shape, and I'm flat as a board, but it doesn't bother me. I'm more than a body. I am a spirit.

It's something no one understands but me. It's something I need to prove to the world. Food is not as important as we think. Man does not live on bread alone.[31]

Or on bread at all, for that matter. I smile in the dark, my nightly ritual of rib-counting over. I can feel them all. Now to find my hip bones.

Black-and-white photos of relatives in old-time clothing hang on the walls of this room. They're lit up by the moon and look like creepy angels. The room smells of mothballs from the trunk holding extra blankets and quilts. I'm here for the summer, just me and my grandparents, in Mitchell, Ontario. A land of corn and cows. I'm hours from my parents and my brother and my sisters.

I've been sent away because home has become a place of yelling and slamming doors. The loud sounds that happen when missions collide.

Mum's mission is to make me eat. Dad's mission is to take care of the church. My brother's mission is to try to fix the family he feels I've ruined. Except he really just misses me. I know this because he gave me a mug that says "You're Beary, Beary Special" when I turned eleven and was forced to stay one week at the Toronto SickKids hospital. It's my favorite mug.

And my sisters, well, their mission is to pray for our family. Sometimes I hear them whispering from the windowsill where they sit together.

After I measure my wrists, I say my prayers. I don't have many words for God these days. Sometimes I don't even think *He* understands my mission. Which is strange because it's spiritual. But one day He will. They all will.

In my dreams everything is angular and dark. I keep bumping into sharp corners.

Naked babies stare at me from a painting on Grandma's bathroom wall. They're warming up by a fire after a bath. Hanging off the towel rack are fancy pink towels I don't dare use, so I grab a towel from the linen closet, which has a laundry chute inside it. After my bath, I step onto the scale. The arrow bounces down, down, and I'm glad. But I have to lean against the counter to catch my breath.

I pull on jean shorts, which hang loose now. My mission here is almost complete. Two months of skipping rope on the deck and taking walks down the country roads. Two months of saying "No, thank you" when Grandma tries to give me toast or meat or potatoes. Two months of success.

I spend most of my time in the dimly lit basement den, lying on the vintage orange couch by the wood fireplace, writing or drawing or reading. Each day, after breakfast, I make my way from the kitchen down the stairs—past the little cubby for tucking our shoes by the garage door; past the doorway to the garage, which smells of cement and diesel, where the car and croquet set are kept; down another flight, past the cold storage full of canned goods, then Grandpa's woodshop, where he spends his time when he's not outside with his antique tractors. I curl up in the den, which is directly across from the tiny bathroom, its toilet perched up high for water flow. You have to climb a small set of steps to reach the toilet. I like that bathroom because it's warm, and I'm always cold. My fingers and feet are forever purple.

It's my final day at the farm, and my parents are coming to get me. Last night I ate five peas for supper. I ate them slowly, peeling off the outsides with my tongue and teeth, then chewing the insides. They tasted like garden and soil. I drank my water slowly, filling up on liquid that has no calories. Guilt-free water.

I look in the fridge now for breakfast. Find a jar of canned peaches. I will eat two slices, but no juice, because there's sugar in the juice.

Food has become my enemy. It keeps me from what's really important.

My spiritual mission.

Every breath has become something tangible, something sacred. I'm sure I am thinking more clearly now that I don't have food to clog up my body.

I am unaware that I'm dying.

For two days now the scale won't dip lower than sixty pounds. It's very frustrating. It seems my body has called stalemate.

I've ceased eating entirely. I stopped eating when we got home from Grandma's, and my parents told me they'd admitted me to the general hospital in Sault Ste. Marie.

There were more of the loud sounds then: of the yelling and crying and slamming of doors. My brother looked sad. My sisters ducked into their room, to their windowsill.

I hid in bed for two days, staring at the yellow curtains fringed with white lace that Mum sewed for me. I stared at the white wallpaper with its bouquets of purple and pink flowers, at the bottle of hairspray on my dresser, at the baptism plaque that sat in my window. It couldn't save me now.

Nothing could save me anymore. The scale had stopped moving. I couldn't cut anything else out of my diet because I wasn't eating. And the mission, though it should have succeeded, didn't make sense anymore.

I was supposed to be entering grade eight in two days. Not going to the hospital.

My friends were planning their back-to-school outfits. I was packing an overnight bag with nightgowns and stuffies.

"You can still study," Mum tells me now from the front seat of the van on the way to the hospital. "I'll bring your assignments from school." She's crocheting, and Dad is driving.

Autumn waves at me from the side of the road, her orange leaves flapping. I don't wave back.

My stomach no longer growls. It's given up trying to be heard.

We cross the bridge over St. Mary's channel, where I once went boating with a friend. We turn left at the corner with the big gray rocks and the Trading Post.

Soon it's Bar River, then Echo Bay, both like aged patches of skin, pockmarked with a few stores and homes. Then it's Garden River, a First Nation reserve. I attended a powwow there once with another friend who's currently taking the bus to school, where I should be going.

My friends will be laughing and talking about their summers and comparing their lunches and giggling over boys. It's our final year before high school. Our senior year.

At some point they'll notice I'm not there. At some point they'll figure out I'm not just the weird pastor's kid with braces and a failed perm. No, I'm the weird pastor's kid who stopped eating and had to be put in the hospital.

We're close to the city now.

That's when I see her. She's jogging along a path. Her hair is in a ponytail, and she's wearing shorts and a T-shirt. Her arms move back and forth, so strong. Her legs, too, are all muscle. A smile is on her face.

She's so very alive.

And suddenly it hits me—how very much I want to live.

The examination table is cold. I'm in a thin hospital gown, and I can't stop shaking. I feel like the color blue. A dozen faces peer over me. Nurses say the word *hypothermia*.

They put me in a wheelchair, take me to a room. Mum shows me my bed and the washroom. I change into a T-shirt nightgown that has cats and hearts on it, and I slide under the white sheet of the hospital bed. Mum hands me Cuddles, my teddy bear. She's crying.

"Sweetie," she says, sitting on the end of my bed in her long jean skirt. Her soft hand reaches for mine. *Please don't go,* I want to say.

Mum swallows. "The doctors say you should have died, honey. They say you're a miracle. God saved you for a reason. Emily, please, won't you eat now? So you can come home?"

Mum leaves. I'm all alone.

I hug Cuddles, but really I'm hugging God.

"They say you're a miracle…. God saved you…."

I keep hearing Mum's words, over and over, like the crinkly ribbon on a cassette tape.

God is more than a plaque in my bedroom window. He's more than the red-letter words in my Bible. He's more than the dry brown cubes of bread or the juice in the tapered Communion cups or the hymns choked out by the pump organ.

He's my Father, and I can finally see Him.

I see Him in me.

I see Him in the freckled skin of my arm. I see Him when I look in the mirror at the girl whose cheeks are so thin they show the imprint of her braces.

I see Him in my bony knees and in the lumpy toes at the ends of my feet. I see Him in this skinny temple of flesh and blood.

I see a miracle. Like a mother looking at her child. Like Mum looks at me.

"Let us make mankind in our image."[32]

One day, I'll learn how the glue that holds our 37.2 trillion cells together—the laminin—actually takes the shape of a cross. How God's love holds us together, cell by cell.

Word made flesh.[33]

"Talitha koum!" Jesus says. *"Little girl,...get up!"*[34] He reaches into the black chasm of death, pulls out life. He takes the dead girl by the hand. She rises.

"Now give her something to eat!"[35] He tells her parents. The God who just raised someone from the grave now becomes very practical. It's as if He takes an origami paper flower and, with one touch, turns it into a real flower with petals and stem and roots. Then He hands it to someone and says, "Now water it!"

This Sustainer of the universe, who makes something from nothing, who says, "Not by bread alone," breaks bread and eats bread.

The nurses bring me a tray of food, and for the first time in four years, I eat everything. I don't try to figure out how many calories are in each item. I don't separate the food, then eat a small portion of one of the sections. Instead I take bite after bite of the fish and the potatoes and the peas and the carrots until they're all gone. I even eat the small slice of cake and the gelatin that shakes like it's happy to see me. I drink the juice. All of it.

And for the first night in a long string of nights, I don't count my ribs.

I spend two months in the hospital. I walk the halls. Talk to God under my breath like the mental patient they say I am. Do my homework.

Clumps of my hair fall out. My purple nails crack and break.

My skin flakes like snow.

I'm shedding death.

I'm not allowed to be discharged until I'm eighty pounds.

Near the end of two months, my friends surprise me. They show up with pizza.

We sit in a room reserved for guests, with faded fabric chairs, a loveseat, and a box TV in the corner. Me in my pajamas and my friends in their jeans and T-shirts, all of us laughing and eating pizza. Our fingers smell of parmesan and parsley. The sun shines through the windows, and it warms us like we're plants in a greenhouse.

I don't remember what we talked about. I just remember feeling the way the jogging woman had looked. So very alive.

The next morning when nurses weigh me, I am eighty pounds. The pizza has done the trick.

I can go home.

oil

The olive tree…is assuredly the richest gift of heaven.
—Thomas Jefferson[36]

2002 – LEBANON/JORDAN

It's easy to believe, here on Mount Lebanon.

I stand surrounded by a thousand cedars of God. The air is heavy, like a hand pushing. It smells like Christmas. I can hear the Spirit in the wind, whispering through branch and needle.

In the Middle East, the *adhan*, the Islamic call to prayer, is a dinner bell. Islam gathers her children five times a day. I find the reminder to pray haunting, beautiful, like the image of Daniel bowed by his window.[37] "*Allahu akbar*," a voice cries over speakers that spit and crackle. "God is bigger."

They worship the God of Abraham but reject Abraham's seed.

I'm twenty-two, engaged to a farm boy named Trent. And I'm on a six-month mission trip.

It's been nearly ten years of eating and dating and laughing. Of Dad taking me to Ann's Café and ordering cinnamon buns, and us getting to know each other. Of sleepovers with friends and road trips and finally getting my period and having my first kiss. Then, Bible school, where the boy with the dark eyes caught mine like a fishhook.

I miss him here among the Christmas trees. We first spoke in the kitchen of my townhouse. It was 1998. He swung long legs from the countertop as he ate pretzels; I stood, awkward, by the sink. We talked about family, about layering up and heading out each Christmas to find the perfect tree.

Then Trent took me home to meet his grandmas and his sisters and his mother and father. We ate strawberries from the garden and lay on the trampoline, staring at the stars.

The cedars point now like fingers to heaven.

I'm here with other missionaries. We climb back into the van, wind our way down into the Beqaa Valley, a place of vineyards and wineries.

I spend my first week in Tripoli with Mathilda and Herman. Mathilda, from Germany, is wiry and tall with short hair and kind eyes. She takes me to the prisons and local markets, touching women gently on the shoulder, leaning in calmly, like she doesn't have three children hanging off her. She teaches me Arabic and patience.

Herman is from Holland. He's thin with a shaggy beard. He rides his bike all over Tripoli. His eyes dance when he laughs, and he can often be found at a coffee shop, ignoring his mug of coffee, hands moving, explaining the gospel to the *shabab*, or young men.

Herman makes Jesus real to me. He wears the same trousers and white-collared shirt every day, it seems, the same open-toed sandals, but when he looks at you, it's like viewing the face of a father seeing his newborn for the first time. Every time.

At night, there's often a knock at the door, one of the *shabab* from the coffee shop. Nicodemus, come to receive.

Sometimes we drive to the olive groves.

The oil drips down my fingers.

A week later, I'm in Warhanieh, a tiny mountain town with white stucco houses teetering on the edge of a valley. We're surrounded by hills, like mounds of dough or a mother's breasts.

Communion is everywhere here: in the flat roofs crawling with grape vines, in the porches of the houses where women sit and cook flatbread.

I live with two other missionaries. Below us is an elderly lady we call *Teta*, or Grandma. She owns the house. When we laugh too loud, she bangs on her ceiling with her stick. Sometimes we go down and eat grapes with Teta. Behind her hijab, her eyes twinkle.

Morning and evening I'm seated on the porch overlooking the valley. I watch the sun rise and fall like a flame of fire. Somehow the sky never burns up.

If I peer far enough it's as if I can see my Lord walking the streets of Tyre and Sidon.

All night while I sleep, I listen to Arabic tapes. All day I listen to God while walking the paths and talking to people.

"*Tfeddali,*" they call from their doorsteps. "*Ahlan wa sahlan,*" they cry. "Welcome!" say these village women who sweep and bake flatbread and hang laundry. It's not often they see a blond woman. They feed me figs and grapes and leaf tea in tiny little "gourds" with metal *masassas*, or straws. This type of tea is called *yerba mate*. We smile and nod and sip it, together.

God lives in the doorways here too.

I move again, from the hilltops of heaven to the sooty streets of Beirut. Everywhere, tall cement buildings are blemished by war. Tired palm trees, looking like plastic decor, line the roads.

On the shores of the Mediterranean, fishermen pull up nets. The city smells like a pair of dirty socks.

But still, the call to prayer sounds.

I live in an apartment with an older missionary, a single woman who reads, drinks tea, and is fluent in Arabic. She is quiet, and I am lonely.

Each morning I take a taxi to my *madrasa*, or Arabic school. Each afternoon I teach English in a Palestinian camp—at a school shoved inside rows of slum houses, packed full of people. The children are smudged with dirt but happy. They don't listen to me. They smile and giggle in their stained blue uniforms. The teachers try to comfort me. I don't understand them.

Every night I continue to fall asleep listening to Arabic.

Every morning I try my language skills again, stopping in at the shops, attempting to talk to the women who sell flowers and dresses. The taxi drivers ask me to marry them. I point to my ring finger, and they laugh. I'm just a way for them to escape their country. They say, "Visa, visa."

On the last day in the camp, I give the children ball caps from home. They raise them high in the air for a photo.

Then I move to the hills, to a city called Aley. The air is cooler here, the palm trees less tired-looking. This pristine Druze city sits on the road to Damascus. I live with other missionaries, and we do church together with Arabic Christians. Many days we order *manakish*—Lebanese pizza, cooked in a stone oven. Sometimes we order it with olive oil and *za'atar*—sesame seeds, thyme, and sumac—sometimes with cheese.

The *manakish* tastes like home.

Here, I teach children who wear clean yellow uniforms. And I teach English to Muslim mothers using the Bible.

Here, I learn to speak in spiritual tongues, even as I learn Arabic.

On November 21, a member of our team is shot three times in the head.

I'd spoken with Beth at a retreat just days earlier. I'd asked her if she had any children. She'd smiled, said she hoped she would one day. Just thirty-one, Beth was a nurse who worked with pregnant Muslim women in a missionary clinic in Sidon. With every birth she'd place her hands on the baby and whisper, "*B'ism Yasua*," or "In the name of Jesus." She'd been opening up the clinic at eight in the morning when she was killed.

A team meeting is called. I walk in, see Beth's husband, Adrian. A dozen people surround him. There's a table laid with food no one is eating.

Adrian is in a cap and baggy pants. He's weeping. He goes around the room and hugs each of us, one by one. Like he's comforting us.

Then he sits and says, "As soon as this happened, a seed was planted in me. I had the choice as to whether this seed would grow into love or hate. So, right at that moment, I chose to forgive."

It's food enough for all of us.

After Christmas I move to Ammon, Jordan, with its dry streets and its lemon trees. Iraqi women sell tobacco on the curb at the bus stop. In the desert, there are huge cacti with red fruit, like plump green hands with painted fingernails. Sometimes the taxi stops to let sheep cross the road. The sheep are slow and stubborn. A shepherd in a turban follows, waving and smiling.

I visit the Jerash Ruins, where the dust from Roman horse races still settles. I eat *falafels* and *tabouleh*—a salad thick with parsley and lemon juice. I play guitar for kids' clubs and do ministry with local missionaries at the University of Jordan.

I tour the Petra and wade in the Dead Sea. My friend dives in, clothes and all. She floats easily in the saltwater.

We camp in the Wadi Rum, the Valley of the Moon, under a plastic tarp. Here we learn the story of the Bedouin tribe, nomadic animal herders. I see the stars so clear here in the desert.

I stand on Mount Nebo. There's a statue of a snake wrapped around Moses's staff. Like the cedars, it points to heaven.

Tomorrow I'll fly home to Canada.

I'm at church now in Beirut, my final Sunday.

I'm here with a family I met five months ago. They invite me for lunch at their home afterward.

We sit, and we eat together, this mother and her five girls.

Suddenly one of the daughters looks at me in my red sweater and my jean skirt. "You've put on weight since you first came," she says.

Everything stops. I put down the bread.

I try to laugh. It sounds like a sob.

All I can hear is the woman saying to my mother, "My, she's a big girl, isn't she?"

I feel very silly and bloated in my jean skirt and red sweater.

The plane ride home is long.

I'm making lists.

Lists of what to eat and how to lose weight before the wedding.

I can no longer hear the call to prayer.

benediction

They had discovered one could grow as hungry
for light as for food.
—Stephen King[38]

2022 – EN ROUTE TO CANADA

Years later, I'm on a different plane, also headed home.

I flip to the indie section on the TV screen. There, a listing for a film that sounds familiar: *Babette's Feast*. The topic intrigues me: "During the late 19th century, a strict religious community in a Danish village takes in a French refugee from the Franco-Prussian War as a servant to the late pastor's daughters."

A stewardess arrives; I order tea.

The plane dips and soars, a white bird. The film begins.

I am immediately absorbed by the story of two beautiful but plainly clothed Danish young women and their somber father, who wears a wide white collar around his neck, like Dad would sometimes wear. I assume there's been a funeral. Everyone's garbed in dark-colored clothes.

Later, when I'm back at home, I read the book by the same name, on which the movie is based, whose original setting is Norway. I learn why these young women wear dark colors—of the funeral that is their life:

> Their father had been a dean and a prophet, the founder of a pious ecclesiastic party or sect, which was known and looked up to in all the country of Norway. Its members renounced the pleasures of this world, for the earth and all that it held to them was but a kind of illusion, and the true reality was the New Jerusalem toward which they were longing.[39]

The father and his daughters and the rest of the congregation would sing about this New Jerusalem:

> Jerusalem, my happy home,
> name ever dear to me...[40]

They would also sing the following, calling to mind my former days of hunger:

> Take not thought for food or raiment
> careful one, so anxiously...
> Wouldst thou give a stone, a reptile
> to thy pleading child for food?[41]

Were the people of this congregation living on stones?

Because of their beauty and grace, the daughters are sought after by suitors, but they set aside any longings to remain with their father and serve their community. "The fair girls had been brought up to an ideal of heavenly love; they were all filled with it and did not let themselves be touched by the flames of this world."[42]

As I watch the movie version of *Babette's Feast*, it pains me to see the dean carry a Bible under his arm, while seeming to have forgotten the lavish abundance of Genesis. He'd forgotten the God who cried, "It is good!" over the pomegranates and blackberries, the oranges and plums, who commanded fruit to have seeds so food would be plenty, trees bursting in blossoming song.

He'd forgotten the love of the Father, how He cares for His people:

> He shielded [Israel] and cared for him;
>   he guarded him as the apple of his eye....
>
> He made him ride on the heights of the land
>   and fed him with the fruit of the fields.
> He nourished him with honey from the rock,
>   and with oil from the flinty crag,
> with curds and milk from herd and flock
>   and with fattened lambs and goats,
> with choice rams of Bashan
>   and the finest kernels of wheat.[43]

Instead of honey and oil and curds, this father and his daughters permitted themselves to eat only split cod and ale-and-bread soup, cooked down until the ingredients were almost unrecognizable.

Much like Communion without the taste.

Is it still Communion, then?

1995 – CANADA

I'm fifteen. We've moved, again, to just outside Echo Bay, Ontario, and we're gathered in the living room. It's afternoon, but the curtains are drawn.

A fern spills onto the piano. House plants crowd every corner.

I sit on the carpet, my brother and sisters on the couch. Mum is in her rocking chair.

Our dogs lie on the landing, and our cat sits on the lap of one of my sisters. The cat is purring, like it isn't the first Saturday of the month, like it isn't family budget day.

Dad is at the easel, writing on a roll of paper—things like "electricity," "heat," "water," and "groceries."

He's on a half-salary now with his new job, preaching at a little white church in the town of Goulais River. He's also taken on a chaplaincy role with Canada's Reserve Force. He's tired and rarely home but still helps me with my math.

He pushes up his wire glasses now. Looks at my brother, then me. Says he's created a little gizmo for our bathroom downstairs. It's a plastic disc with tiny holes attached to the showerhead to slow down the water rate.

I'm getting an allowance now, but I have to provide everything for myself: shampoo, deodorant, clothes. I buy my clothes from the thrift store. Last week, I used laundry bleach to try to dye my hair. My scalp still itches.

While Dad's talking, I'm sketching, working on handmade greeting cards. I'm going to sell them at the local gift store in Bar River. I've also got a job selling Watkins and Regal products door-to-door. I'm saving up for real hair dye.

We're reminded not to touch the thermostat, to put on more layers instead. Each morning, at breakfast, orange juice is limited to half a glass, homemade granola to half a bowl. Lights must be turned off before leaving a room, or we will be charged. And if we want to use the dishwasher instead of washing dishes by hand, we will need to pay seventy-five cents. The clothes dryer is to be reserved for emergency situations.

"What about towels?" I ask. "Can't we put them in the dryer? They're so scratchy when they hang on the line."

Mum's rocker pauses.

Dad shakes his head.

The rocking resumes.

There's a pro-life rally this weekend after church. We're all expected to attend and hold the signs.

We might stop afterward to get day-old donuts.

Dad says we're dismissed.

I open the curtains. Sunlight is free.

Part Two:

The Feast

table

If you don't feel strong desires for the manifestation of the glory of God, it is not because you have drunk deeply and are satisfied. It is because you have nibbled so long at the table of the world. Your soul is stuffed with small things, and there is no room for the great.
—John Piper[44]

2017 – SIERRA LEONE

It's my first time in Lungi. The island caps Sierra Leone like a green beret.

I step from the plane to meet a man I don't know, a man I've only talked to through WhatsApp. I've spent most of the flight praying.

There's a flurry of suitcase-grabbing and visa-checking and young men eager to carry my luggage and get a "tip."

table 81

That's when I see him: The man with the towel draped over his shoulder.

"Welcome to West Africa, ma'am," Ibrahim says with a smile, his tongue thick with a tangle of French and English called Krio. He mops his shorn head with the towel. Shakes my hand and grabs my bags full of dresses and ties and diapers and old pairs of glasses and other things people donate for Africa.

I feel safe.

A year ago we learned about Ibrahim after a forty-day period of fasting and prayer. A new contact on Facebook reached out about him: said he was a good man, had a heart for God, was caring for orphans, and I should speak to him. I knew nothing about Sierra Leone.

We take the sea taxi now across the Atlantic with her frothing girth. After forty minutes, we reach Freetown, a city named for the slaves shipped to its banks and told to form a country. Ibrahim tells me that former slaves from Canada cleared the land in 1792.

We climb into his army jeep; a paper flag striped green, blue, and white hangs from the cracked windshield. We drive through the night, through city streets paved by the Chinese. We pass nightclubs and phone stalls and fruit stands and countless young people walking the streets arm in arm or hand in hand; women seated on the curb with babies, selling bananas and watermelon, trying to make enough money to feed their families. I smell charcoal and motor oil.

We slow by a tree in the city center, the Cotton Tree, ascending like an anthem from the asphalt; she spreads her branches like a mother saying, "These are my children."

Ibrahim tells me a lieutenant ordered the slaves to clear the land until they reached this tree. After the land had been cleared, the tree remained, and all the women and children and men, with preachers in front, marched toward it, the preachers singing, "Awake, and sing the song of Moses and the Lamb."[45]

Such a triumphant procession, this army. Poor but free. Having nothing but knowing the One who owns everything.

We drive past the beaches now, past the sand and the tourists. "I sold plastic packets filled with drinking water, each day, on those beaches, during the civil war," Ibrahim says.

He tells me stories of witch doctors and demons, how it's not safe for children to walk the streets at night—some are taken as human sacrifice. He says demon worship is so bad you can sometimes see spirits flying across the sky like witches on broomsticks. He says female genital mutilation is a common practice in the villages.

I want to cry.

We reach Ibrahim's house, just three small rooms. Attached to his house are other small houses. They're painted brightly, as if to say, "We're okay! Don't pity us!" His wife, Mariama, greets us. She's a buxom woman with smooth skin and a firm jaw. She's cooked us fish, battered and crisp; mashed potatoes; and boiled *matoke*, or green bananas. Children from the streets eat with us. Ibrahim and Mariama aren't able to have kids of their own.

We sit at a table in a room partitioned by a curtain. I have to turn sideways to squeeze past the kitchen. The bathroom is a shared toilet outside—only one for the whole block of brightly painted houses.

"One day we will have a home large enough to fit everyone," Mariama says.

The next day we wind along red-ribbon roads like a bobbin of thread—finally halted by what seem to be hundreds of villagers.

table 83

Wrinkled, walnut faces press to the windows of the jeep, bodies wrapped in bright African cloth. There's the sound of singing: schoolchildren marching in unison in blue uniform, led by "Aunt Adama," the village nurse, a tall, slim woman with a large smile.

Everywhere, lush green leaves, grass as high as my head, bananas hanging ripe and coconut trees with trunks like ancient brown scrolls. The world has become a fruit basket.

We inch into the open. The women move to the front of the vehicle. Their faces crack wide with smiles, and they're swaying and dancing. The children cheer and march. Men run alongside with machetes. They've been cutting the long tails of grass, clearing the way for "Daddy" Ibrahim.

"Hello, hello, hi," they sing into the windows, then chant a chorus in Krio I don't understand.

This is a country with no reason to rejoice.

This is a country still reeling from Ebola, mass graves hiding bodies, orphans wandering the streets looking for home.

It's a country losing hundreds of people each year to floods and witchcraft and poverty. And yet they sing. Like the men and women who marched toward the Cotton Tree, they sing.

A thousand tongues singing their great Redeemer's praise.

Ibrahim parks by the farmhouse. This is his father's village, and even though Ibrahim was raised in the city, one day he woke up, remembered the ones left behind. The forgotten villages.

So this pastor returned—and continues to return, year after year—to help his people. He brought what little he could, spent what he had, and prayed for more.

Near the farmhouse, a bamboo structure has been erected, overlaid with palm leaves; it is filled with rented plastic chairs. The imams and sheiks and priests of neighboring villages are here. It's the first time a foreigner has entered the village of Masaralie in the

Kambia district, and they tell me if I come again, I'll earn the title of chief.

I'm in a T-shirt and slacks, no makeup. Yet I feel like a queen. Like grass, adorned.

They bring me a fertility drink and a goat. I've never been this close to a goat before. His eyes dart; he seems to know he'll be eaten.

They ask for a speech, and I rise. Tears fill my eyes, like my heart has turned to water. If only they knew how sinful I am. Yet love covers.

I stumble over my words, find some.

"I'm here to be your friend," I say. "We need you like you need us. We need to learn from you. So let's start now," I finish, soft. "Let's begin to share." I gesture to my heart, then to the sky. "I love you because Jesus loves you. Thank you."

They clap, an explosion of hands.

Even though I've been on other stages, this one is the finest.

We're in a restaurant at a table for three. I can't eat.

Ibrahim calmly selects a chicken dish from the menu. Mariama chooses fish. They both look at me. I swallow, point at the cheapest item: rice. Ibrahim's eyes twinkle.

It's the last day of my first trip to Sierra Leone. We've just been to the Kroo Bay slum, one of the worst slums in the world. We've seen boys do backflips in a garbage dump. We've seen a little girl seated outside her home, one that balances on the edge of the slum's toilet—a piece of land filled with human excrement. We've seen other girls wearing cheap makeup, and preachers who live in cardboard houses.

table 85

Now Ibrahim has taken me to the finest restaurant in Freetown. He knows I have no money—I've run out of cash, and it turns out my credit card doesn't work here. Ibrahim also has no money, he says. And yet he has brought me here.

He says he wants to teach me something.

I figure we'll have lots of time to learn something in prison.

A waiter comes, and we order food we cannot pay for. I can barely sit still. Ibrahim keeps chuckling.

The food arrives.

I force down the rice; Ibrahim and Mariama take their time as they talk together and eat their meals.

Finally, the bill.

Ibrahim tells the waiter his name, then asks him if his friend is around. His friend, it turns out, is the owner of the restaurant.

No, the waiter says. The owner has left for the day.

My heart sinks.

Ibrahim nods. The waiter leaves.

Suddenly he returns, says he's called the owner, and the owner is coming.

Eventually the owner arrives, engages us in conversation. Then he says, "Well, thank you for coming! Have a nice day," and he starts to go.

All of a sudden he turns back. Grabs the bill.

"I'll take care of this," he says.

But for God.

Ibrahim thanks him and we leave.

Outside he turns to me.

"Now, don't you wish you'd ordered more?" he says.

bread

*Good bread...smells / of its own small death, of the deaths /
before and after.*
—Margaret Atwood[46]

2003 – CANADA

My homemade bread is holey, like it forgot to rise in the
middle, like it was making room for a miracle—only the miracle
never happened.

So instead we eat holey bread.

Or rather, Trent eats holey bread. I drink coffee. Here in our
kitchen in the basement. We're newlyweds.

Big slices of white flesh with giant circles in the middle. The
peanut butter and jam slide through onto the plate, a messy puddle.
Trent quietly mops it up.

"Sorry, babes," I say into my cup in a low voice. The coffee stares up at me like a brown teary eye.

"It's okay," he says. He takes a swallow of milk.

The space between us is wide.

I've made bread since I was seven, but somehow it's like the bread knows I'm empty now too, drinking coffee all day and eating only supper.

Sometimes supper is a bag of marshmallows at 4:45 p.m., to fill in the space the miracle is supposed to go. Because I can't quite wait until five, and yet I won't let myself eat until then. So I stuff in the marshmallows, white powder on fingers and lips, while I paint—gobs of acrylic on canvas, covering every blank space with color.

I cry one night when Trent puts butter on the popcorn. It's movie night, and he just sits on the couch with his bowl of buttered popcorn while I make another bowl without butter. I try to sprinkle on the salt. It falls off.

"Why don't you just eat mine?" Trent says. He sounds like he's in a tunnel. But his leg is warm against mine. We're like shaky apostrophes.

We chew in silence. My popcorn is dry.

"That He might fill all things."[47]

Sometimes I remember the olive oil, the tiny cups of sugar tea, and the grapes, tangled thick and purple on flat rooftops.

"That you may be filled with all the fullness of God."[48]

"I'm in the Bible these mornings with my coffee. The sunlight a wedge of lemon in the glass of our basement window. I'm in Ephesians. It's like the food is right in front of me, but I can't eat any of it.

I don't know how to eat God. Do I crumple up the pages, put them in my mouth like Ezekiel with the scroll that tasted sweet?[49]

But I don't. Because I'm stuffed full of marshmallows. Sugar and air. I'm glutted with man's lies.

The voice that told me I was big is louder than the Voice that says I'm dearly loved.

Yet I can't stop reading. Marshmallows only fill for so long.

These delicate, translucent pages bear the weight of salvation. They say His love knows no depth nor height nor width, like the hands that stretched wide across eternity, nailed to our sins, to our skins, to our skinny understanding of His big, big love. But how easily ripped, these pages. How very fragile, this life.

Trent and I still find each other beneath the sheets, and he smells like earth and spice. On our wall is the photo of our married-day, of the white arbor in my parents' backyard, of the circle of fake flowers in my hair. If crushed, they would have smelled like plastic.

But children scattered real rose petals on the grass after we said our vows, and we danced across them, hand in hand, and the crushing smelled sweet. Then we gathered under a long white tent with a potluck of tiny sandwiches and potato salad made by church ladies.

Mum baked the cake, double-layered and iced yellow. On top was a bride with a goofy smile, gripping the black tailcoat of a groom trying to get away.

If I were him, I'd try to get away too.

On weekends we sometimes go back to the farm, a fall drive lined with square patches of gold wheat and bright-yellow canola, a quilt sewn with seed and sod.

If only you could patch up holes with light.

At the farm we lie on the trampoline, stare up at the stars like we used to. His hand finds mine, and I'm glad it's dark because I'm crying.

I know what I'm doing. I've done it before.

I'm listening to the naked brain in *A Wrinkle in Time*. The evil IT.

And I long for Mrs. Whatsit and Mrs. Who and Mrs. Which to come and make everything better again.

1991 – CANADA

Auntie Gladys was my Mrs. Whatsit.

"I give you my love, Meg. Never forget that. My love always."[50]

Auntie Gladys and Uncle Joe grew love like they grew trees on their acreage by the river. They found us tousle-haired on the front pew of their church at Hilton Beach. They welcomed us and took in my Mum too, and my Dad, and I've never seen my parents happier. Like they were kids whose cheeks had been smothered with kisses.

After tea and cake at Auntie Gladys's, we'd leave the dishes, move into the living room.

Auntie Gladys would hold one of us kids on her lap while Uncle Joe pulled out the fiddle. He'd spend a few minutes tuning and then...

"On a hill far away, stood an old rugged cross...."[51]

Dad's tenor mixing with Mum and Auntie Gladys's sopranos, Uncle Joe's bow gliding across the strings in a living room covered in doilies.

It's like we got all stitched up at Auntie Gladys and Uncle Joe's. Like their house was a sewing machine, and they were really good at mending.

Auntie Gladys's kitchen was small, but we were never in her way. She always wanted us closer—to help her bake, to tell her stories, to make her chuckle.

"Come tell me more, Emily," she would say. "How is school? How is English?" She knew I loved language arts most. Auntie Gladys was a retired schoolteacher, and she'd push up her silver glasses and smile her wrinkled smile. Love became a cozy place in her kitchen.

Time was somewhat wrinkled, too, in that home, almost like a tessering. We'd go to bed when we wanted and eat when we wanted and laugh all the time. I'm sure I even laughed in my sleep.

"The fullness of him who fills everything in every way."[52]

God became flesh, became Uncle Joe with his twinkling eyes and his suspenders, Auntie Gladys in her apron.

"They saw God, and they ate and drank."[53]

And even as I stopped eating whenever I wanted, and I began to disappear, Auntie Gladys and Uncle Joe kept hugging the space I used to be. They kept inviting me to the table.

2006 – CANADA

My soul is hollowed out like holey bread.

Trent tries to hug the space where I used to be. I cry in his arms as he falls asleep.

This is year three of marriage. The days are long, blank spaces filled with coffee. The nights are even longer.

I leave the bed, curl up on the couch once again, try to rest once again. It's like trying to add yeast after the bread has already been made. I know this isn't a fast. This isn't something spiritual; it isn't a mission. This is purely flesh. It's a hunger strike. I just want to be thin.

As much as I'm still reading the Bible I'm not digesting anything. I am nibbling, maybe, then spitting it out, as if Scripture might be fattening. And then I wonder why I can't hear Jesus anymore.

Somehow, even though this isn't spiritual, I know everything, deep down, is.

I think of the faith of the Syrophoenician woman. She desired a whole loaf but settled for crumbs. Because she knew God could do with crumbs what He can do with an entire loaf.[54]

The Syrophoenician woman was humble. "The root word of humble and human is the same: humus: earth. We are dust," Madeleine L'Engle says. "We are created.... But we were made to be co-creators with our maker."[55]

Dust, the milling of wheat berries into flour.

But I'm the berry that clings to the stalk.

I don't want to let go.

The stalk has been cut down with a scythe, and yet I cling.

They say that to remove the berry from the stalk, the farmer needs to slam the wheat, over and over, against the inside of a bucket.

Finally, when the berry releases and falls to the bottom of the bucket, it is winnowed. This is where the light berries blow away. The farmer grabs the berries that have fallen and drops them in front of a fan, and the heavier berries fall to the bottom of the bucket. The lighter ones blow away with the chaff.

I'm so light now I might be winnowed away. Am I but chaff? Nothing of substance?

Most nights now, I rise from the couch and type out prayers like poetry into a blog. My one subscriber, a friend, always responds with kindness.

Sometimes I'll then climb the stairs to my attic gallery and pour paint onto canvas, trying to feel the brightness of the colors. When I run out of canvas I begin to paint the slanted ceiling.

Finally I'll take a sleeping pill and press my face into the cushions of the couch.

We're on a highway between Calgary and Edmonton when the letting go happens.

It's been a weekend of visiting friends in Calgary. I took too many sleeping pills the night before because I couldn't sleep at all. I didn't wake until noon. Trent got scared.

We've been fighting the long ride home. I have no more strength to hold on. I'm driving, and I simply turn the wheel toward oncoming traffic. This might be where I blow away.

"Emily! What are you doing?!" Trent yells. He grabs the wheel, pulls us to the side of the road.

We've both fallen, berries bumping into each other at the bottom of a bucket.

All of a sudden I remember the tree.

I was standing on a hill overlooking the city of Aley when I had the vision. It was one of the first times I saw something without my physical eyes. I saw a tree, a big rambling tree, like a wood nymph from Narnia, full of branches and fruit, and I was in the tree, on a branch, holding on. I was trying to grab the fruit but couldn't because I was too busy trying not to fall.

"Just let go," I heard.

My knuckles were white.

"You won't taste the fruit until you let go," the Voice said. It was a kind voice, like Auntie Gladys's or Mrs. Whatsit's, a voice of love.

"Truly, truly, I say to you, unless a grain of wheat falls into the earth and dies, it remains alone; but if it dies, it bears much fruit."[56]

In the vision, I eventually fell.

And these huge, divine hands, like a farmer's, caught me.

When the fruit fell, ripe and round and ready, I could finally catch it. Because my arms were finally free.

Piles and piles of fruit in my lap. And I ate. Held up by the winnowing hands.

We sit at the side of the road now, cars whizzing by like crayon streaks of color, and I cry.

My face falls into my hands, like my neck has given up, and I just weep. Finally, I look up at Trent through my fingers.

He is staring out the windshield. He doesn't cry, but his chin looks frightened.

Then he turns to me, this man who dressed in his army uniform the first day he asked me out, like he knew it was going to be a battle. Who brought me daisies, who couldn't find the words to say. Who still smells like musk, the same cologne he will use for twenty years from the same bottle. He turns to me now.

"Emily, I can't do this anymore."

My head is so heavy. My hands push it up to look at him. I force myself to see him. This man with the hazel eyes who's waited so long for me to come back to bed.

"I've been patient," he says. "I've waited for you to come around, but you're not, and I can't just stand by and watch you die."

He swallows, his Adam's apple sliding.

"I need you to choose," he says. "I need you to choose between me and food. Because if you choose food, I'm out."

We once kissed in the rain. We ran out into the storm from his old townhouse where he lived with a bunch of college friends, and we stood beneath the weeping sky and kissed.

We officially broke up for a year and a half because we were too young to get married, and yet we kept meeting in secret. Because Trent's mouth was something special. He never flattered me. He only ever spoke truth. When I told him I wanted to be a news anchor, he said, "Why? Is that what God wants you to do?" Unlike the other boys, who said I would be good at it because I was pretty.

"Mercy and truth are met together; righteousness and peace have kissed each other," the psalmist says.[57]

After eighteen months, we prayed about getting back together.

I heard God say this was the man He had prepared for me.

Trent heard God say He was giving *him* the choice.

Now Trent's handing the choice back to me.

I call Heaven and Earth to witness against you today: I place before you Life and Death, Blessing and Curse. Choose life so that you and your children will live. And love GOD, *your God, listening obediently to him, firmly embracing him. Oh yes, he is life itself.*[58]

God Himself. My life.

"They are not just idle words for you—they are your life."[59]

A scroll to be eaten.

I stare out the window at the long road. I remember the ride to the hospital those many years ago. The woman running. The doctors murmuring, the blue dressing gowns, the shivering on the examination table, the smell of Lysol, Mum saying I was a miracle.

I should have died.

I need to get out of the driver's seat.

I look at my shy soldier.

"I choose you," I say.

2006 – SOUTH KOREA

Unless the wheat berry falls, it cannot be turned into flour. It cannot be anything but a seed.

I'm climbing a mountain in Korea, surrounded by temples. They call it Chiaksan. Trent and I climb it often, and always the same man is hiking, as he does every day, in bare feet. He laughs when we pass him, his face full of a thousand lines like a thousand rivers.

"I like to feel the earth beneath my feet," he says.

We've left everything to start over. It's a rebirth, this coming to Asia, a land of spiced cabbage and rice, a land of women selling colorful fruits and veggies on the side of the road. We ride a red scooter here, and we live in a little apartment with a balcony. Our *apartu* is beside the *sobongso*, or fire station. Sometimes we look over the balcony and see children laughing while watching a fire station demonstration. Sometimes we see *adjumanis* and their grandchildren drinking tea or taking a taxi to Emart, Korea's superstore. Always we see the tree that guards our front lawn like a sentry.

Behind our apartment is another mountain, a smaller one, and we hike that one too and make silly faces together into the camera. I eat three meals a day here, slowly and carefully at first, and then with a smile, until I am laughing like the man with a thousand rivers. Because the food here is healthy. I can eat until I'm full, and there are no marshmallows here. Just beef broth and seaweed wraps and rice. Sometimes I make big salads. They don't sell croutons here. I love croutons, so I make them.

I make food matter by making croutons. I buy a loaf of white bread, cut off the crusts, cut the slices into cubes, sprinkle olive oil on them, toss them with some seasoning salt, then lay them on a tray, bake them in our toaster oven.

We teach English to Korean children and play games with them, and something else begins to stir, even as I am reborn.

My holey heart is being filled with a miracle. A Voice of love woos me like Hosea's wife is wooed in the desert.

"I will…speak tenderly to her…. And she will sing there…."[60]

"There's a filling up happening. And I'm finally sleeping again. Love and rest intertwined, like arms.

When I was thirteen, I picked up the fork and ate, and I gained enough weight to go home. I stuffed away the old life, and I went on dates and dressed in funky clothes and attended concerts and tried to forget the hunger years.

But there was still a part of me that was left starving. The soul part.

Now I am a baby again, held by giant divine Farmer hands. I am breathed on by the Winnower. I fall into soil, into dust, from where I came. To be planted, again.

It is a quieting time.

Sometimes when I stand on Chiaksan, I hear the Father singing over me. Rejoicing over me. This sinner of a girl.

I need to feel the earth with my skin. Humus. The flour-dust that is our skin.

What grows in the soil feeds our bodies. The soil is our bodies. We are but crumbs.

"I will plant her for myself...; I will show my love to the one I called 'Not my loved one.'"[61]

There's a responding happening—between God and sky, sky and earth, earth and grain, grain and Jezreel,[62] for we have a God who sows. A divine conversation, and I can finally hear it, like a collision of voices, a symphony of love, and it's all happening inside me, the vacant place becoming a concert hall.

And even as I'm reborn, drinking Ephesians like it's milk, with words like *"he chose us"* and *"we have redemption"* and *"to the praise of his glorious grace, which he has freely given us,"*[63] the hole inside me is finally being filled.

Holey bread turned holy seed.

wine

Christ knew that by bread alone you cannot reanimate man.
If there were no spiritual life, no ideal of Beauty, man would
pine away, die, go mad, kill himself or give himself to pagan
fantasies. And as Christ, the ideal of Beauty in Himself and
His Word, He decided it was better to implant the ideal of
Beauty in the soul. If it exists in the soul, each would be the
brother of everyone else and then, of course, working for each
other, all would also be rich. Whereas if you give them bread,
they might become enemies to each other out of boredom.
—Fyodor Dostoevsky[64]

2007 – CANADA

I'm feeding Mum like she's my child. It's pea soup from a can, her favorite brand.

She has a yellow cloth napkin tucked into her collared shirt, the pink-and-blue shirt with ivory buttons. It takes her a long time to do up the buttons. She sings while she does, sitting on the edge of her bed, and sometimes she forgets what she's doing and just lifts her hands and worships.

Each morning when I climb the stairs, I see Dad in the TV room, kneeling on the carpet, having his prayer time. He does it every day.

Later, at 10:00 a.m., I'll hear "Mocha Time" coming from the computer. It's Dad's voice pre-recorded just in case he's in a meeting or had to step out, so Mum knows she can have her mocha.

Mum has a brain tumor.

A month ago, while I was still in Korea, Dad texted me, told me Mum's cancer had gotten worse. He asked me to watch Mum over the webcam so he could go to a meeting. That's when Trent said I should go home.

Mum was having headaches before our wedding. The kind that felt like the thorns in Jesus's crown must have felt pressing into His head. They did surgery on her right frontal lobe, and now she's missing part of her brain; yet somehow the cancer is still growing.

I go home.

It's May, and I won't see Trent until August. He's finishing up our contract teaching English. He sends me pictures of him eating yummy Korean food and flying to Thailand with just a passport, a toothbrush, and a pair of boxers in his fanny pack. "Love you, babes," he writes.

I can still smell the cherry blossoms.

Mum's blue eyes follow my face. I smile, and she smiles. Soup dribbles down her chin. "Are you done now, Mum?"

She sighs. "Yes, I'm just not that hungry these days," she says in her British accent.

Then she smiles. "But I'll have dessert now, please."

I laugh. "Mum! You have to finish your lunch first."

"You're right, Emily. You're absolutely right."

My mother, the nutritionist, who snuck zucchini into our chocolate cake and made homemade granola every day, now has a wall hanging that says, "Life is short. Eat dessert first."

"*I die every day!*"[65] Paul says. But in this dying, we live. In the falling of seed is the rising of new life, drinking in light and rain.

Bird feeders hang by the dining room window. Mum and I bird-watch as we sit together. The flashing of color, the dipping of beaks, the feeding on seed they did not strive for. Mum's eyes dance, and the light shines in.

Jesus could have been performing miracles right before He died. Instead He chose to have one last supper with His friends.

Maybe eating together is a miracle.

"*I will come in to him, and will sup with him, and he with me.*"[66]

Even as I wipe Mum's mouth, I remember days of cod-liver oil and food charts. I get her pills. She spends the next hour trying to take them. By the end, she's tired, and she leans on me as I help her up, and we walk toward her room. A worship song is playing on the CD player, and she stops. Closes her eyes, lifts her hands, begins to sway. It's like she's already halfway to heaven.

> *The body that is sown is perishable, it is raised imperishable; it is sown in dishonor, it is raised in glory; it is sown in weakness, it is raised in power; it is sown a natural body, it is raised a spiritual body.*[67]

I tuck Mum into bed, pull the covers to her chin. She grabs my hand.

"I love you, Em. You are so beautiful."

I rise from darkness into light.

The Spirit that spoke something into nothing is speaking into me.

In the beginning was sound. The sound of the Word, separating and gathering, emptying and filling. The sound of God stirring up depths and summoning forth life. "Because the Holy Ghost over the bent / World broods with warm breast and with ah! bright wings," says Gerard Manley Hopkins.[68] The sound of a happy Father, announcing the birth of His creation.

There was the flap of feather, the trumpet of elephant, the squawk of more new things forming. Upon waking I'm sure they heard the laughter of God. And I wonder if stars leaped then, from His mouth into the sky, the Son leaning down and whispering to the dust, *"Let Us make man in Our image."*[69]

Up rose gangly limbs and toes, like yellow-fluff chicks learning to walk on giant claw feet. Man and woman. Clumsy and perfect.

Brushing soil from skin, they blinked, saw rainbow light, the beaming face of their Abba.

Woman, born by God, one day to give birth to God. Woman who sinned. The holy, become skin in the womb of the world.

God must have pointed then to the trees He'd planted, to the garden, watered by underground streams, to the blackberries and papayas and peaches. *"I give you...food,"*[70] He said.

And just as He made man, aged, and tree, aged, perhaps God opened a skin of aged wine as He will on the mountain in the greatest of feasts, because the next day was the first Sabbath. Feast day. The blood of His Son poured out, even before the creation of the world.

Even in their perfect state, human beings needed to eat. Yet eating would ruin their perfect state. All for a piece of fruit.

And soon the sound of the Father's laughter would be replaced by the sound of Jesus weeping over Jerusalem.

The Creator become the Created, become a baby wrapped in swaddling clothes.

It's been said these "swaddling clothes" were, in fact, more than a soft baby blanket. Rather, they were strips of thin, gauze-like cloth travelers wrapped around themselves before a journey. The purpose of the cloth? To bury the sojourners' bodies in, should they die before reaching their destination.

With no other cloth available, it makes sense that Joseph, a recent sojourner, unwrapped his own swaddling clothes and used them to cover the Christ child.

If this is so, what a sign—this baby, wrapped in his father's swaddling clothes, laid in a feeding trough. Food for the world, this infant born to die.

He came to feed the multitudes, yet they did not repent. Time after time He gave them bread, yet they demanded more. Perpetually empty.

"Eat Me, then!" He cried. "Drink Me!"[71]

They decided to silence Him instead.

It was the plan all along.

He, the living Bread, to be broken at the Feast of Unleavened Bread. His side gushing wine for the nations.

A table of suffering. A holy Communion.

And then, in the night of the tomb, like the yeast that feeds off dead or decaying organic matter, His body rose. The Bread rose in the dark, folded His swaddling clothes, and wrapped Himself in light.

"Listen, listen to me, and eat what is good, and you will delight in the richest of fare."[72]

I'm rising now, too, from the earth, all gangly limbs and toes, this awkward seed feeling the sun for the first time. God is feeding me, like He fed Ephraim, lifting the yoke from my neck and bending down like a mother bird to put morsels in my beak.[73]

I'm relearning food, even as I will relearn God for the rest of my life, this Father Creator who pours out sunshine and rain on insignificant seed, so tiny and small. Yet He sees it. He sees me.

And it is good.

But then there are days the darkness lingers.

Days when I climb the stairs and Mum doesn't appear.

Dad greets me, instead, with a hug. "She hasn't woken yet," he says.

And we just look at each other. Because at any moment, Mum could slide all the way into heaven. Swaying to the chorus of ten thousand angels.

I enter her bedroom. It's dark and smells of unwashed sheets. Mum's face is pale on the pillow, like a squeezed-out teabag. I miss the blue of her iris. The quilt rises and falls over her chest like a quaver or an eighth note. I touch her hand, and it's cold. I tuck it under her blanket.

"Mum?"

Nothing.

"It's Emily. Your 'favorite daughter.'"

I'm trying to make her laugh.

Still nothing.

I sit on the side of the bed, begin to sing quietly.

Great is Thy faithfulness, O God my Father....

It's pure obedience, this singing, yanking up my spirits like I pull up Mum's pants some days.

There is no shadow of turning with Thee;
Thou changest not, Thy compassions, they fail not;
as Thou hast been, Thou forever wilt be.[74]

Then, from the bed, a stirring. A moaning, dry lips parting.

"Mum?"

A soft crooning; she sings, "Great is Thy faithfulness, O God my Father...." Still, her eyes remain closed.

She won't wake for the next eighteen hours.

That evening I grab my guitar, go to the store, buy a bottle of wine, head to the beach.

I sit on the sand with the seagulls. They croak out songs like it's worship hour.

Then they rise with an ecumenical prayer, off to their next service.

I listen to the laughter of the waves.

Drink straight from the bottle. Write a song for Mum.

I am here to witness.

I witness the soft cushion of sand composed of a billion tiny rocks. The wisp of cloud sliding like a silk blouse across the pink abdomen of sky. The weave of a bird, stitching together the horizon like a needle, and the long thread of an airplane behind it. I witness silence, which becomes a thousand compositions of sound the quieter I get.

And I witness the waves splashing.

"They knew Him," my young son will tell me, one day. "Even when no one else recognized Him, the waves knew Him."

In the love feasts among the Corinthian believers, people acted in a way that "[despised] *the church of God.*"[75] Today we have such agape feasts, with their egg salad sandwiches and gossiping mouths. The hungry poor outside the doors while the fat became fatter in the foyer of the church.

But that is not what I find this time.

This time my dad's church is not some tall, redbrick face that seems to glower down on people and dare them to climb its steps. Only to find the doors locked.

This time Dad's church is a school gymnasium streaked with marks from the soles of kids' shoes.

Each Sunday my dad and his elders arrive early to lug in the worship stands and sound equipment. Each Sunday Dad erects a flimsy music stand as a podium, and then they set up the chairs. And if there's a potluck afterward—or a "potbless," as Mum would call it—then they pull out the folding tables.

Dad then drives home to get Mum, whom I've helped to dress. She'll often still be trying to take her pills as she sits in her jean skirt with the buttons down the front. She'll have her purse and her Bible, and she'll have a bit of white residue from the pills on her lips. Sometimes I'll dab light pink lipstick on her mouth. Then Dad and I will help her to the car, and we'll drive a few blocks to the school.

We are the hungry poor. And we're feasting together, witnessing God together, in torn leotards and plastic chairs.

As Fulton Sheen writes:

Broken things are precious. We eat broken bread because we share in the depth of our Lord and His broken life. Broken flowers give perfume. Broken incense is used in adoration. A broken ship saved Paul and many other passengers on their way to Rome. Sometimes the only way the good Lord can get into some hearts is to break them.[76]

We still drink juice. But we do it different now. We rise, row by row, make our way to the front, where the elders stand holding a loaf and a single goblet of grape juice. Mum toddles behind me, gripping my shoulder. Together we pull off some flaky bread, and I wonder if I'm taking too much—how much of Jesus's body am I supposed to take? How much do I leave? I don't want to be like those greedy people in the Corinthian church, keeping the food to myself, yet I want to truly taste Him. Then we dip the bread in the juice, and it stains purple, even as we bring Jesus to our lips. His body, His blood, one loaf, one cup. Sometimes our fingers stain purple too. It feels more eternal that way, more lasting.

We make our way back to the plastic chairs, Mum humming a tune, me thinking about Christ's seamless garment, how even as the soldiers grabbed it, tore at His tunic, it wouldn't rip. How Satan grabs at the church, pulling and stretching it, but in the end we remain one garment. One loaf. One goblet. Consumed, poured out for many, yet never used up. Never finished, because *it is finished*.

We sit. Mum plays with her purse, and I ponder Jesus thirsting. "*I am thirsty*,"[77] He said in His final moments, in the fullness of His humanity, with the sole purpose of fulfilling Scripture. Perhaps because He didn't want His final words to be missed. He wet His throat so all the powers and principalities could hear Him declare, "*It is finished*." [78] Even as He died.

He thirsted so we might never thirst again.

The worship team begins to lead us. Mum rises awkwardly to touch heaven with her soft palms, her face lifted and eyes closed like she's asleep on God's chest. This is a good day. Sometimes we have to bring Mum to church in a wheelchair because her legs won't work right.

We sound a bit like the seagulls, but it's holy somehow, like the juice, like creation, in all of its dying and being reborn.

> They have no speech, they use no words;
>   no sound is heard from them.
> Yet their voice goes out into all the earth,
>   their words to the ends of the world.[79]

Mum doesn't do a lot of talking now, but her silence is a sermon to me. In the way the volcanic mountains swallow their power and point instead with granite fingers to the One who made them. In the way the bush simply burned. It didn't beg. In the way Jesus hushed the waves.

The kingdom of heaven does not belong to flesh and blood.

> There are also heavenly bodies and there are earthly bodies; but the splendor of the heavenly bodies is one kind, and the splendor of the earthly bodies is another.[80]

It's the slip of the fish into the net, the seed into the soil. It's that space between something where I'm learning how to pray. That sacred place of rest and powerlessness. It's the same kind of quiet that hovered over the waters at creation.

A silence that hovers over all of our souls, and breathes.

Trent comes home. We purchase a little white house across from the gymnasium church.

All those years of not eating have carved out a womb so big doctors say it is the penthouse of wombs. But it is vacant, and they say it will stay vacant. They say starving has stolen my babies. I can't have children.

But a pastor disagrees. His birth was an answer to prayer for his mom, so he prays for us, that we will conceive a boy within a year. I nod politely.

The stick turns pink, and I believe in miracles.

A few weeks later I miscarry. I decide miracles are overrated.

Meanwhile, I'm still drinking tea with Mum and folding her laundry and watering her plants. We have her and Dad over for supper twice a week, and again I feel very much like a mother already.

And then it happens, on Valentine's Day. Within a year of the pastor's prayer. And this time, the seed sticks. This improbable, impossible seed somehow grows into a boy, springing to life from a simple prayer. From faith as shaky as my mother's legs.

Around this time my Mum shows up on my doorstep. Alone. Beaming, her eyes like cornflowers.

She has walked all the way from Bible study on Main Street, all by herself. She didn't get lost, and she didn't fall down. "Surprise!" she says, and laughs, then collapses into my kitchen chair.

A sweaty, blue-eyed wonder.

Shortly afterward, doctors say the remaining parts of Mum's tumor have disappeared. They can't find them anymore, and they won't, for the next ten years.

Even with thirty-six hours of pushing and bleeding, it remains a miracle. This filling and emptying of womb.

I didn't know I could give birth to love. Love has long eyelashes and his father's hazel eyes.

And there's the sound of a happy dad declaring his son's arrival, and soon another emptying, even as this sweet-faced baby, all gangly limbs, fills up on my milk.

Mum is able to hold him, us helping her. Months pass, and this seed becomes a contented, smiling toddler who leaps from a bouncy swing in our doorway and gnaws on wooden spoons and learns how to walk.

But aren't we all learning how to walk?

We who are bone-dry. We who are the prophesied-over:

I will make breath enter you, and you will come to life. I will attach tendons to you and make flesh come upon you and cover you with skin; I will put breath in you, and you will come to life. Then you will know that I am the LORD.[81]

The Creator stretches epidermis over us like a wineskin. Breathes life into us so we can pour out His Spirit.

May we, like the waves, recognize Him. He is Lord.

mangoes

*I want everything, everything, every bit of intimacy
this flesh-and-blood human being can have with the flesh and
blood of Christ.*
—Francis Chan[82]

1982 – NIGERIA

I've been told the story so often, I can almost remember it happening.

I was two years old. I had on my favorite T-shirt, the one with a pink bow at the neck, and I wore a cloth diaper fastened with sharp pins and a plastic pullover on top.

My white legs stuck out of the diaper like two peeled bananas. It was too hot for pants there in Nigeria, so I toddled around like this, quite proud of myself.

Mum brought me along with her to visit a local family. Their house was small and dark, and Mum said there was a little girl inside who was blind. She said the girl had never been outside before. Her parents hid her like she was some kind of mistake. While Mum chatted with other adults beneath the trees, I stepped into the house. I could see the girl, in the corner, folded up like one of Mum's letters, stamped and ready to send to Grandma and Grandpa. All creased and pressed, like no one had taken the time to read her yet.

As I got closer I could see she was wearing a dress with pretty pink flowers on it.

To communicate, I most likely made a "hmm" sound with my throat because I couldn't talk yet. It would have been an attempt to sound like Mum when she comforted me after a scary dream.

The girl's legs and arms were brown and skinny, like what people carried on their heads for firewood.

Perhaps I saw the shape of the door shining like a white rectangle on the floor and thought, "I have to get her to the light." I must have known she needed to be in the sun. That's where things grow.

Somehow I found her sandals and helped her step outside. When Mum saw us, she called my new friend "Solange." Later I learned this name means "angel of the sun."

Before we left, Mum took a photo of Solange and me. In it, my hand is wrapped around one of Solange's wrists, and her eyes are closed.

There we stood—she without sight, I without words. Both of us growing together in the light.

2014 – CANADA

It feels like my hands are still wrapped around the wrist of Africa.

I've just returned home from my blogger's trip. Nothing makes sense anymore. There's something in me that needs to be birthed. It looks much like a pile of twigs in a flowered dress.

"No one can see the kingdom of God unless they are born again."[83]

All I've ever wanted was to catch a glimpse of God.

I remember those nights as a child, trying to imagine a face on Him.

It wasn't that He didn't have a face. I just couldn't see it.

This God who shoves aside clouds and sky, who rides the cherubim down to earth,[84] who puts on human feet and steps into my darkness, who gives me a pair of shoes and pulls me into the light so the flowers on my dress can grow. This God.

I see Him now, as I saw Him in my skin on the hospital bed.

I see Him now, as I saw Him in the mother with the starving baby and in the genocide widow.

God, in *us*.

Open the ancient letters, He says. Read the words scribbled on flesh and bone. Know *Me*.

The woodstove breathes, all pine and smoke.

Outside, snow falls, and my boys and Trent are tucked in bed. As I have done every night since coming home, I'm here in my flannels, on my knees, on the polka-dot rug by the stove. Praying.

In the sorrow, He meets me.

I fight judgment. I fight the sight of my kids' toys, piled high, plastic toys they never even play with. I fight their whining because they don't want supper. I fight commercials and the grocery store and even church.

Most people in North America don't know seven-year-olds can look like three-year-olds because they haven't eaten enough. They don't know *jajjas* (grannies) with crooked backs are picking through garbage. They don't know babies are dying because their mothers don't have milk.

But God knows.

And suddenly He is more than a name in a Book. He's more than a Divine Idea. He's more than theology or a golden, flowing image in a movie.

God is fire and roaring and weeping. He's humanity, but He's also otherworldly, like the four living creatures covered with eyes in the book of Ezekiel.[85] God is limitless: He's found in the whooping cry of a *jajja*, in the face of a man who's seen too much suffering, in the baby left by its mother at the bottom of a latrine, in the mother desperate enough to leave her baby there. He holds all of them.

And He holds me.

He's there, and He's here, and He's the closest friend I have in the world because He's seen everything I've seen, only He's seen it for centuries. He's heard every story I've heard, and so many more.

He's real. *He's real.*

We hear the Bible stories, we know they're right, we're afraid of hell, Jesus sounds like the truth, we repent, we do the altar call and the devotionals and the Bible studies.

But do we put our hands in His side, in the shattered skin of His wrists, touch this real flesh, real blood, eat this real food and wine?

It's the great gap that caverned me as a little girl, swinging my legs from a pew in my dad's church. Feeling the flutter of the Spirit, then sensing it slow, seeing that moment of grace fall, lifeless, to the floor because of people's apathy. Hearing the gasp of pregnancy in the pages of Scripture read from the pulpit—then listening to that pregnancy sputter and miscarry as we walked to our parked cars, to our private, cushioned lives.

I lie prostrate now before the burning bush of the woodstove, like I need to take off my shoes and socks and throw it all into the fire. I want none of it. I am filled with a love too big for my chest.

I'm in the position of traditional birth, like when Elijah travailed to bring rain to the land.[86]

And one night I hear Him.

His voice is a soothing sound, a hug in the dark.

He says, "I have called you."

I cling to these words like I clung to Solange's wrist. As if it had been her leading me all along. As if she could see, all this time.

The combines hum, a harvest choir outside my kitchen window. There's the *slice, slice* of wheat and barley, even as I measure the flour.

Seven cups of water, three tablespoons of yeast, and half a cup of sugar puddle at the bottom of the bowl. My boys sit at the counter. They giggle, mouths full of peanut butter.

I wipe the smudged recipe card with a cloth. It's my mother's recipe.

The air smells of a musty, earthy place of dark and growth, where roots tangle and life stirs.

It smells of the living organism that is yeast, which is everywhere, on skin and soil, yet can't be seen until a million microorganisms clump together, to work together.

It smells of Communion.

Downstairs is the pop and fizz of Trent opening a bucket of homemade wine, the swish as he mixes the fermenting liquid. Then the clatter of glass as he rinses bottles. Tonight we will bottle mango wine.

The bread is kneaded and hides now, like a secret, beneath the towel. The yeast is eating now, feasting on sugar, and the stomach of the dough expands.

My belly, too, is rising. Six months after I returned from Africa, we conceived. Recently we learned it's a girl.

The boys play with scraps of bread-flesh, their middles tied with oversized aprons. Flour freckles their faces, and their little fingers press the dough, smushing and flattening. They beg for raisins and peanuts to hide inside the folds, and then they beg to bake the dough, and so we do.

But it's the making that is the miracle.

The loaves have risen. They are not like the Jewish *matzo*. No, they're round and large, even as they bake, the boys watching them through the lit-up glass of the oven window like it's television. Then we pull the bread out, and I butter its tops.

I think of the exodus, of the preparation of unleavened bread— bread made in haste, without yeast. Those tiny microorganisms that lift an entire loaf, that ferment a bucket of wine, forbidden to the Israelites during a sacred time of year.

We slather hot slices with butter and strawberry jam, and I ponder some of the Jewish feasts.

The first, the feast of the Sabbath, a weekly celebration of divine rest.

The next, Passover, with its unleavened bread, or *matzo*, remembering how God delivered His people from slavery and death. The bread of affliction. *"Father, forgive them,"*[87] the final Passover Lamb cries. The last stanza of the cross, but do we listen?

Finally, Pentecost, in which people brought to the Lord a bread that did contain yeast. They laid down the haste, the fleeing, the un-leavening of the exodus, and they entered into the peace, the abundance, the leavening of heaven.

From wherever you live, bring two loaves made of two-tenths of an ephah of the finest flour, baked with yeast, as a wave offering of firstfruits to the LORD.[88]

I see them now, priests in white robes like bakers in white aprons, singing and waving the bread like palm branches.

Centuries later, during this very same feast, this Pentecost, intercession rose like the bread. Jesus's followers were locked inside the Upper Room, terrified, praying. Suddenly a feast of language was spread for them. The Jews visiting Jerusalem heard their feasting and thought the disciples were drunk. They didn't know a windstorm had swept fear right out of that room, flames of fire consuming everything but zeal. The Word burst from those locked doors into all the nations like Jesus bursting from the grave. And all because Jesus's followers had sipped from the chalice of heaven.

Our boys are in bed now, the bread in the freezer. It's time to bottle wine.

We sit on the linoleum kitchen floor, chat about the day, me holding the bottles and Trent the straw-like hose. The bottles fill, then Trent clamps the hose, corks the bottles, and I stick on labels.

And all the while we're listening to the sounds beyond our window, the whir of the combine-symphony, the songs of the late-night harvest.

The rest of the household is asleep. I'm here, sitting on the carpet in the living room, in the semidarkness, scribbling notes. A candle flickers.

It feels as if God is growing inside of me, as if His newborn foot is pushing against the insides of my soul. Something more than my daughter is being birthed in me. Something spiritual. A new ministry.

And just as we have a special name for our little girl, God's given me a special name for this mission. It's "The Lulu Tree." *Lulu* in Swahili means "pearl"—the very treasure I'm searching for. *Tree* comes from the parable of the mustard seed.[89]

When I put the words together and do a web search of "The Lulu Tree," it turns out there is an actual tree by that name native to Africa. The "lulu" tree, or shea nut tree, stretches wild across the entire midriff of the continent, growing fifteen feet high and taking forty to fifty years to mature. It typically grows in places ravaged by fire. And it will eventually produce shea nuts. These nuts, the website says, are harvested at the exact time of the villagers' seasonal hunger.

You have been a refuge for the poor,
    a refuge for the needy in their distress,
a shelter from the storm
    and a shade from the heat.[90]

All I've got is a mustard seed, but unlike yeast cells, we don't need a million of them. God can take that single seed and make a kingdom.

And that seed feeds on Scripture. My Bible is always open now, and I'm flipping and searching.

How sweet are your words to my taste,
    sweeter than honey to my mouth![91]

I've received a call to help the poor. I'm hungry for instruction.

My soul is consumed with longing
    for your laws at all times.[92]

I think of Brother Yun, often referred to as "the Heavenly Man." At sixteen, during Mao's Cultural Revolution, Yun came to know the Lord. Longing for a Bible, he prayed for a hundred days and fasted, begging God for a copy of His Word. One night God gave him a vision of men bringing him a freshly baked bun. When Yun put the bun in his mouth, it became the Word. Early the next morning, the men he'd seen in his dream came to his door. "Are you bringing the bread to me?" Yun asked them. "Yes, we have a bread feast to give you." They handed him a Bible and disappeared. Yun slept with that Bible on his chest, walked with it under his clothes, memorized one chapter a day until he could carry the Word in his heart, and no one could ever steal it from him.[93]

Come, all you who are thirsty,
    come to the waters;
and you who have no money,
    come, buy and eat![94]

They're seated here with me now, in the Spirit, at a table of suffering: Africa's mothers and their babies. They come and they sit, and I weep over their stories and pray, and Jesus serves them. The finest of things, on a tablecloth of gold, in the quiet corners of my house.

Go out quickly into the streets and alleys of the town and bring
in the poor, the crippled, the blind and the lame.... Go out to
the roads and country lanes and compel them to come in, so
that my house will be full.[95]

I have no idea how to do this, or what *this* is, but His Word is enough. I never wanted to read the Bible before. Now I crave it.

Scripture fills me and leads me because my eyes are now open. I see the lost. I understand the Great Commission. My job is to feed.

But first, to feast.

By day I'm pinning diapers to the clothesline and potty training and teaching ABCs. By night I'm in the candlelight, listening.

I have stretch marks on my soul because of all the intercession. Papers, strewn everywhere, with ideas and thoughts and words of inspiration. But there is not actually anything to them at all.

Nothing except Jesus, here with me. Which is everything.

Oh, to love Him as Saint Thérèse of Lisieux did in her short, twenty-four years. "If, supposing the impossible, God Himself could not see my good actions, I would not be troubled," she writes. "I love Him so much that I would like to give Him joy without His knowing who gave it."[96]

As my baby develops within, growing fingers and toes and a button nose, I long for more. I long to drink from the chalice of heaven.

People slowly join me in The Lulu Tree mission. We form a motley group of mothers, praying in the after-hours. As we pray, we begin to fast. I don't fast from food, but rather from coffee and social media. We empty the soul to feast, more, on this living Showbread.

The poor, pulling us into the light.

fish

*And He departed from our eyes so that we might
return into our hearts and find Him there.
He departed, and behold, He is here.*
—St. Augustine[97]

2018 – UGANDA/SIERRA LEONE

The mamas are many. The day, hot.

A miracle happens.

It happens outside Jinja, Uganda, at the dorms where we house teenage mothers who are going back to school.

It happens with the expectant mothers in the wide-open space between the redbrick dorms and the piggery.

Ivory tents rise high like a wedding canopy. Blue plastic chairs are laid out in rows, having been carried on the backs of *boda bodas*, or motorbikes. And the pregnant mothers sit, row after row, in colorful cloth, some wearing hijabs, others rosaries, others scarves around their heads. The teenage mothers walk around in school uniforms, giggling to each other. Caterers cook lunch at the outdoor kitchen. Large metal pots, hanging over charcoal fires, hold fish sauce, rice, *matoke*, and beans.

I've flown to Uganda with teammates. We arrive at the dorms at nine. The mothers have been coming since sunrise.

The pastors in their white-collared Lulu shirts scribble down names on lined paper, registering each mother as she arrives. At one point my friend Amy asks to see the names. Later she confirms them, line after line, starting with the last name, ending with the first.

The chairs fill. The gate to the compound is open, and village children stream in with big smiles, eager to see the white *muzungu*, or foreigners, and the bulging mamas in bright colors spilling out of the tents, like flowers overflowing from a vase.

The praise team arrives, and the dancing begins. Our Ugandan director calls it the "Blessed Mama Dance." The women sway in the heat with their pregnant bellies, some of them so ripe they look like they'll split open in the sun.

The air smells of charcoal and beans and sweaty bodies. Occasionally the leaves on the banana trees stir. Mostly they hang limp.

We stand on a makeshift stage overlooking the crowds of women, trying to move our arms and legs in awkward dancing. Finally the women pull us down with them, and there is laughter and the twirling of skirts, the whirling of colors.

There are eight hundred mothers surrounding a pile of five hundred maternity kits.

The kits are simple, made up of things we take for granted. Without them, though, no Ugandan mother can give birth within a hospital. The kits contain two plastic sheets (one for the woman to lie on, one for the medical items), surgical gloves, a bar of soap for washing hands, a roll of cotton, new razor blades to cut the umbilical cord, gauze for wiping the baby's eyes, a suction bulb for cleaning the baby's airway, and a swaddling blanket to wrap the baby in.

This isn't our first mama kit outreach. There have been others in the slums and refugee camps, with hundreds giving their lives to Christ. But never have we had so many mothers compared to kits.

The dresses continue to sway and the preachers preach and the women fall on the ground, shaking, because demons come out in the open here in Africa. The delivered mamas lie still as corpses, only to rise and keep dancing. This is Africa.

The night before the outreach we'd prayed a small prayer, not knowing what a big prayer it actually was. We'd asked God to bless, to multiply, the mama kits, but the word *multiply* was like an afterthought, like a kiss on the back of the head. There was no travail.

I'm not even sure we knew what we were asking. I'm not sure how much belief there was behind the word *multiply* because it was just a nice word we chose, more like a "Bless you" after a sneeze. A gratuity, as if God depends on our vocabulary or even our prayers.

In America, if we pray for a miracle and don't get it, we go to the doctor. Or to the pharmacy. Sometimes we pray for a miracle en route to the doctor or the pharmacy.

In the villages of Africa, people pray for a miracle because without it they will die.

Now it is time for the meal. We've purchased enough rice and beans for five hundred people. Not eight hundred, plus village children.

But the caterers dig deep into the pots and pile the plates high. And we help serve the plates to the children and the mamas.

"I saw it with my own eyes," Amy tells me later. "At one point, when I went back to get two more plates to hand out, I looked into the pot, and it was empty. It was *empty*. Yet she, whoever was serving, reached in with her mug and came out with a full mug of food. And that continued for at least two more rounds, because another woman was behind me the second time I went through, and she said, 'There's no food in there.' And I said, 'I know—there was no food the last time I came through. But watch what happens.'"

Every mouth, filled.

And then, time to distribute the kits.

Our director tells me she can't even look. She turns away because she doesn't want to see women go without.

A pastor grabs the clipboard, steps toward the kits; he asks Amy to come and help him hand them out. One by one, he calls out the names. One by one, the mothers come, taking at least one kit, sometimes two if they're having twins.

I watch, and the pile doesn't go down. My friends watch. They also say the pile isn't going down.

We reach the end of the list of names. Still, mama kits remain.

The math doesn't add up. We'd packaged five hundred mama kits. Eight hundred mothers registered. Some even took multiple kits.

Yet somehow 118 kits are left over.

It's a story I've heard since I was a little girl, this one of the loaves and fish.[98] It's a story of Jesus on the hillside with the thousands, breaking bread and fish and feeding stomachs. It's a story that happens twice in Jesus's ministry, one with five thousand people being fed, and the other with four thousand being fed[99]—one with the

Jews, and the other with the Gentiles. Neither number includes women and children.

Our story, however, is all about the women and children.

Finally the white tents empty like a sigh, exhaling dresses and rosaries and hijabs and bellies. The caterers pack away stainless-steel pots, the charcoal fire is snuffed out, the tents are taken down, and the plastic chairs are stacked to teetering heights on *boda bodas*.

Yet the kits remain. A pile of miracles.

Enough for another outreach.

This thing, this seed, which used to be nothing at all, has become a small nonprofit. And over time The Lulu Tree is planted in multiple places, run by mothers who have never done this kind of thing before.

I rise each morning to hug my children and kiss my husband and try to figure out what it means to be the president of something. At night I bow low, thrown down by my smallness and God's greatness, the train of His robe filling my home.

This place of Ezekiel.

This place of Isaiah and John.

This place of seraphs with six wings, who continually cry, "*Holy, holy, holy,*"[100] a Sanctus, which is why we come to worship. The whole earth, filled with His glory. Laying our crowns down with the twenty-four elders.[101]

This place of windstorm and fire, flames moving back and forth between the living creatures as if ignited by the coal that touched Isaiah's lips. The eyes on the wheels turning all around and rising then falling—and over them an icelike expanse, a rush of wing and water, *"like the voice of the Almighty, like the tumult of an army."*[102]

No eye has seen this One who lives in unapproachable light, yet I glimpsed the Man made of glowing metal—*"the Son...the radiance of God's glory...the exact representation of his being"*[103]— and for this *"I fell facedown."*[104]

Trembling with Ezekiel.

And Moses.

Oh, how kind He is to put up with our handcrafted tabernacles, our half-hearted prayers. This transfigured One, this canopy of cloud. This One with the jasper and carnelian and emerald throne. He who is a slain Lamb, with seven horns and seven eyes. He who is Word yet still writes in a scroll to unroll when the hour is here.[105]

May we not refuse Him who writes and speaks.

It's as Lewis describes in *The Last Battle* through the voice of the Unicorn:

This is the land I have been looking for all my life, though I never knew it till now. The reason why we loved the old Narnia is that it sometimes looked a little like this.... Come further up, come further in![106]

This is the land I've been looking for all my life. And so we go further up, further in.

As we pray and fast for the poor, God rises like the Lion He is, and He roars, and hearts and mountains move. People begin to give. We don't ask them to, though we do share the vision of mothers in Uganda.

We have never, and will never, ask for money, nor will we as a North American board take money for ourselves.

Instead we go to the hidden place, to the place George Müller and Hudson Taylor and Amy Carmichael went, and we ask our Father. For isn't it all His? And does He not delight to give it to us? And does He not tell us to ask in secret, and to "not worry, little flock"[107]?

Through much bumbling and sighing and crying and belligerence, I've learned that God is much like Aslan, who says, "You do not yet look so happy as I mean you to be."[108]

How can one not trust a God like that?

"It is a safe thing to trust Him to fulfill the desires which He creates," says Carmichael.[109]

And when I read in *The Last Battle* of swimming up the Great Waterfall, "till it seemed as if you were climbing up light itself"; when I read of, one day, running with the Eagle and never growing weary in a world where the color blue is *more* blue; when I read of Aslan himself "leaping down from cliff to cliff like a living cataract of power and beauty,"[110] I'm sure nothing is impossible.

Except for sometimes when I rise from the carpet and check our bank account.

And then there's the bumbling.

There's the time when I go to a local market to advertise The Lulu Tree. I set up my table and my pamphlets and my cards, and some hand-sewn items to sell from a friend who wants to support the ministry. I sit there all day.

Despite the crowds, I collect a total of twenty dollars. I gather my things and go home. Everywhere is drought. I drive past fields that look like balding men, thin strands of canola rising from dry scalps.

Trent has taken the kids to visit his parents. I step into a quiet house, leave everything in a pile, and fall to the floor. I don't say anything—I just weep to my Lord.

And I hear Him say, "Daughter, yours is not to sell or to bring in money. Yours is to pray, and Mine is to provide."

When you're starting, and you're so small, every moment feels like it will make or break you.

But I crawl into Jesus's heart and visit His love for the poor and for me, and I believe. In His love for us.

I choose to believe I am loved. I choose to believe the Big Word instead of the little words. The Word who looks at me with eyes that most definitely have laugh lines.

And even as we mothers meet online to pray and then head offline to make supper, I ask God how to do this. This loving of others. This serving alone in the quiet place, the loveless place, the dry place. Straining our eyes, like Elijah's servant, for the tiniest cloud.

I am praying for a "battle plan," and God gives me Gideon's: it consists of trumpets, some weapons, a timid leader, and a few brave soldiers against a huge army. And God gets all the glory.[111]

He also speaks to me of Moses. When the Israelites left Egypt and reached the Red Sea, Moses told them, *"The Lord will fight for you; you need only to be still."*[112]

And God said, *"I will gain glory for myself."*[113]

So I'm raising my staff and trusting the Lord to provide for all our needs. To stir in the hearts that need stirring. To fan the flames that need fanning.

I'm trusting Him for loaves and fish.

~⌐

Heidi Baker and her husband, Rolland, are missionaries in Mozambique. I've been following their ministry, Iris Global, since my university days.

In their book *There Is Always Enough*, Heidi writes about experiencing weakness. She'd been caring for over three hundred orphans and was becoming increasingly exhausted and ill. She'd been on antibiotics six times in two months; then she got pneumonia.

Most people would have gone to a hospital. Heidi went to a revival meeting.

She left Africa to attend an awakening happening at the Toronto Airport Christian Fellowship, and God spoke to her when she was deep in prayer:

> One night I was groaning in intercession for the children of Mozambique. There were thousands coming toward me, and I was crying, "No, Lord. There are too many!" Then I had a dramatic, clear vision of Jesus. I was with Him, and thousands and thousands of children surrounded us. I saw His shining face and His intense, burning eyes of love. I also saw His body. It was bruised and broken, and His side was pierced. He said, "Look into My eyes. You give them something to eat." Then He took a piece of His broken body and handed it to me. It became bread in my hands, and I began to give it to the children. It multiplied in my hands. Then again the Lord said, "Look into My eyes. You give them something to drink." He gave me a cup of blood and water, which flowed from His side. I knew it was a cup of bitterness and joy. I drank it and then began

to give it to the children to drink. The cup did not go dry.
By this point I was crying uncontrollably. I was completely
undone by His fiery eyes of love. I realized what it had cost
Him to provide such spiritual and physical food for us all.
The Lord spoke to my heart and said, "There will always
be enough, because I died."[114]

Then there's the tractor.

Never in my life have I purchased a tractor; nonetheless, it is
needed in Sierra Leone to plow land to provide food for eighteen
villages, and I wonder how to go about getting one.

We kneel to pray, and a name comes to my mind. It's someone
I've never talked to. A contact on Facebook. All I know is, she is a
farmer, but the Spirit tells me I need to write to her.

I send her this simple message: "We at The Lulu Tree are looking at investing in a tractor for our Sierra Leone farm, and I was
wondering if you know of any discounted tractors or have sugges-
tions on where we could start."

Turns out, the state this woman lives in, California, had just
instigated an emissions-reducing program, urging farmers to
replace old tractors. So this woman and her husband reach out to
the state government, tell them about us and our work in Sierra
Leone, and ask if they would consider donating a tractor.

The government of California says yes. They will gladly give us
a tractor. A 1995 Kubota with 81 horsepower.

This couple and their church then proceed to ship the tractor,
filling every empty corner of the shipping container with clothing
and shoes and supplies.

Months later I'm present to witness the arrival of the tractor in the village. We make a procession through the jungle. It's a slow procession, the red Kubota leading the way, the palm trees waving their leaves, and the villagers whooping and cheering. It reminds me of Jesus entering Jerusalem on a donkey.[115]

And even as we drive the winding path to the village, I glance down at the tattoo on my wrist. It's of lilies, and it reminds me God will take care of the lilies—so how much more will He take care of us. How very much more.

She with the lost coin doesn't rest until that coin is found.[116] He with the one lost sheep leaves the ninety-nine other sheep to find it.[117] He with the prodigal son waits expectantly at the end of the road for his son to come home. And when the son finally appears—this one who'd shamed his father, who'd spent all his inheritance, who only returned because he was hungry—the father runs down the path, sweeps him up in a hug, then commands the servants to *"bring the best…"*![118] He covers this shamed one in the finest of robes, lays out the richest of foods, throws the most lavish of parties to celebrate his son's return.

God's love is not an economic metaphor.

Sometimes we think of love like a commodity, like money. We keep it from those who do not agree with us but lavish it on those who do. It sounds like a smashing together of two cymbals.[119]

But our God's love is a "free-gift" metaphor. He lavishes kits upon mamas and food upon children. He knows no other way to be. Like a waterfall knows only to gush water.

Oswald Chambers says, "If love is always discreet, always wise, always sensible and calculating, never carried beyond itself, it is not love at all. It may be affection, it may be warmth of feeling, but it has not the true nature of love in it."[120]

I'm Martin Luther, exposing the heresy of my own former doctrine—nailing it to the door for all to see that righteousness is not something good or right that I do but simply belief in what God has done and will do.

This God who is love.

oil

*We must be careful not to choose, but to let God's Holy Spirit
manage our lives. We must not smooth down and explain
away, but rather "stir up the gift"…; we must allow God's
Spirit to disturb us and disturb us and disturb us until we
yield and yield and yield and the possibility in God's mind
for us becomes an established fact in our lives, with the rivers
in evidence meeting the needs of a dying world.*
—Smith Wigglesworth[121]

2018 – CANADA

My daughter is singing in the sand, making castles with her
cousins. One of her brothers is in a kayak, and the other has just
caught a fish. We're camping at Lesser Slave Lake. I pick up my
phone to take a picture of the pike when I see my sister's text:

Mum's health has rapidly deteriorated and Dad's taken her to emergency. The doctor is saying we have less than a month left. The intern says days.

My mother-in-law takes the picture. All I can think is, "I have to go home."

Home for me used to be a place far from my parents.

At eighteen, I took a bus for forty hours from Ontario to Alberta, a Chippewa man asleep on my shoulder.

I moved in with girls I didn't know, and we all attended a tiny Bible school in Edmonton.

That's when the farm boy grabbed my hand. He took me to the country, to the long stretch of field, to the weathered barn and the rectangular garden, to the cow pasture and the river running through it, to the trees where he would one day carve our initials. He took me to his house, with its lilac smells and its brass dinner bell, and I learned grace there, at the kitchen table.

His mom asked what I wanted to eat: "Anything you want, I'll make it, and please, eat until you're full." I didn't know how to answer. And when she asked me how I liked my eggs—yolk broken or not, easy over or sunny-side up—I stammered. I'd never been asked before.

Food is sacred on the farm. Food is fed. It is milked and grown and named, sprung from the belly of the earth as if attached by an umbilical cord.

"Farming is united with the agape, the love feast, the Mass, for liturgical worship and food go together," writes Catherine Doherty in *Apostolic Farming*. "Farming is an altar on which only the bread and wine of truth can be placed."[122]

Bread on the farm isn't just a loaf in a pan. It is a wheat field. It is hours in the sun spent tilling up soil, fertilizing, planting, and praying for rain and heat; and then it is harvest—the combine and the truck weaving rows into the night, until the wheat is threshed and sold to become flour to become bread to feed the world.

"As I cover the ground with my footsteps, I spread my prayers," writes apostolic farmer Scott Eagan. "I am increasingly aware that, through my baptism and as partaker of the Eucharist, I carry Christ into these fields."[123]

At the farm table, grace is more than a prayer. It is heaping spoonfuls of thick cream and chocolate cake. It is meat, nursed as a baby, grown to maturity; young potatoes, soil-dusted from the garden. It is peas from the vine and carrots and lettuce, grown and loved. It is tall glasses of milk from a cow who has a name. And then it is a card game and chips and dip and ice-cream floats.

Love is incarnate there.

I know this because the first night in Trent's home, I smashed his family's chandelier.

We'd been playing a fast-paced card game at the kitchen table, and I'd been winning. I rose in triumph, punched the air in victory; in so doing, I punched the light. The fixture fell, a thousand shards of glass.

The thing is, I hadn't met Trent's mom yet. She'd been gone when I arrived.

She soon came, and I approached her, sobbing, but she merely hugged me and laughed. Said she'd been wanting a new light fixture anyway. Then she bandaged my hand and swept up the glass.

"The inclusion of sinners in the community of salvation, symbolized in table fellowship, is the most dramatic expression of the ragamuffin gospel and the merciful love of the redeeming God," writes Brennan Manning.[124]

This God-Man who looks up and says, *"Zaccheaus, come down immediately. I must stay at your house today."*[125] This God-Man who comes eating and drinking, called Glutton and Drunkard.[126] His feet, bathed in oil by a woman whose only name is Sinner, yet what she does will never be forgotten, Jesus says.[127]

Because a meal is communion. A sharing. Pass the bread, pass the butter, partake of grace.

The Jewish people understand this. As Manning writes, a Jew will welcome a true companion by saying, "Come to my *mikdash me-at*, the miniature sanctuary of my dining room table, where we will celebrate the most sacred and beautiful experience that life affords—friendship."[128]

We become children at such tables, ready to receive.

My husband and I fly from Alberta to Ontario the morning after getting my sister's text. Then I hail a taxi for the two-hour drive to my parents' home.

I'm in the passenger seat of the cab, stuck in traffic, when I get another text.

Mum has died.

My only prayer has been, *"Please let me say goodbye."*

Sometimes it feels like God is laughing at us.

The taxi driver sees my tears, offers me some figs. They taste like dirt. I don't tell him.

Finally we're at my parents' house—two hours too late. I give a Bible to the taxi driver. He fed me, I feed him.

Then I go inside.

Mum isn't Mum anymore. She's just a lifeless doll lying there cold and white and bloated, but her clothes still smell the same. Strange men come and take her away, and I cling to her pink collared shirt like it will save me. I don't wash her clothes for a week because then I'll wash away my mother.

Dad hugs me. He's still warm and very alive. He says, "Sorry."

"It's not your fault, Dad," I say. He nods.

Then I run to the backyard, to the dry grass and dandelions, to the soil. Soil is skin, is life, is genesis, and somehow, next to Mum's shirt, it's the closest I can get to Mum and to God. It's as if God's heartbeat lies just beyond the epidermis of the dirt. I press my face to His heart. Dust to dust. Like there's a hidden door here, and if I become small enough I can pass from this life to the next.

"All are from the dust, and all return to dust."[129]

I wonder if this is why Jesus knelt in Gethsemane, a place that means "oil press." This garden where oil was squeezed from olives, perhaps used to light the very lamps that shone day and night in the temple.

Jesus pressed Himself to the earth. Sweat, like blood, squeezed from His forehead.[130] No doubt He was trying to feel His Father. *"Take this cup,"*[131] He cried. An angel strengthened Him. Jesus took the cup, filled high with the pain of the world, and drank.

He offers it now to us.

Mum is laid out at the funeral for everyone to see. I want to scream, *"This isn't really her!"* But grief is funny that way. The green olives fighting the press.

I put a teddy bear in the coffin with Mum.

One of my sisters sits at the piano. We stand up front as a family with our guitars and our mics, and we sing.

We sing the song "Anástasis." The name means "rising up" in Greek. Scientifically, the word refers to "a natural cell recovery phenomenon that rescues cells from the brink of death."[132]

Resurrection. The great rescue.

But first it's a song about death, about Jesus's wounds and His bloodied hands and feet, and I think again of Gethsemane, the garden at the foot of the Mount of Olives. That place of pressing.

I think of the cup filled with tears, filled with sorrow. I think of Jesus begging His Father to take that cup but adding, "*Yet not my will, but yours be done.*"[133] I think of the water that will flow in the last days from the temple in Jerusalem. Zechariah says the water will be "*living,*"[134] like the water flowing from the temple in Ezekiel, making everything new again. Trees springing up on both sides of the river to heal and to feed the nations.[135] Much like the garden of Eden.

And even as the ground swallows Mum's body and the teddy bear, and it feels like everything is gone, I think of the feet of Jesus planted firmly on the Mount of Olives in the final day. Zechariah says the place of Jesus's agonized prayer will become a place of triumph. The battle He won privately in the garden will become a very public declaration of victory—His resurrected body rising from the ridge of the Kidron Valley, the mountain splitting from east to west, the nations defeated by the sword in His mouth, this very Word of God.[136]

All these places of pressing will become places of rescue. The cross making an open spectacle of death.[137]

We go home then to the "*house of mourning,*" and grief feels like the mouth of the ground, swallowing; I take to heart the inevitability of death, like King Solomon tells me to,[138] but I don't sleep well for weeks. My mother was like a cord that attached me to the earth. When I lost her, it felt like I was floating.

Somehow, though, this house of mourning becomes "*a house of feasting.*"[139] As Warren Wiersbe says, "Sorrow can be like nourishing food that strengthens the inner person."[140]

Every smile becomes courageous, like the skin of a farmer. A testimony to life and death. And even as I forget Mum's scent, I begin to smell heaven. Because Mum is more alive now than ever before.

2015 – UGANDA

Africa is another house of mourning.

Africa, with her babies dumped in the trash.

I receive a text from our Ugandan team saying they've found a three-day-old baby wrapped in a polyethylene bag, thrown in the garbage in the slums. The baby is still alive.

The text appears in the same style of font we'd use to say, "How are you doing?" or "What's up?" Only instead, it says this unthinkable thing.

We name the baby Treasure because that is what she is. This baby, likely birthed on a dirt floor in a shack in one of the eight slums in Kampala. She's still unwashed from birth, still has blood on her skin, a sweet girl grown in a warm womb for nine months, then pushed into a world that didn't want her, bagged and tossed.

A local children's home takes Treasure in.

When you're born in dirt, and you live in dirt, you begin to believe you are dirt.

Forgetting of course that dirt is God's medium of choice. It's what we're all made of. It's what Jesus spread on the blind man's eyes to make him see.[141]

And even as I bow at midnight, weeping for all the babies wrapped in plastic, Jesus tells me to become poor.

To become poor and needy before Him. To get low, to press deep into the pain of Treasure's mother, to carry her suffering to the cross, where He holds all mothers and their babies in His crucified hands.

Sweat, like blood, in a garden.

Then I see Him. In the quiet of the night, I see Jesus.

He's so big and filled with light. He's so tall, He rises above the ceiling. But then He shrinks and becomes very emaciated. A child, skin and bones.

He grows again, so tall, majestic, filled with fire, but soon shrinks again, and He's got shorn hair with lice crawling in it. Finally He rises once more, to glorious heights, then shrinks one more time, so tiny, and I look down and see His feet: they're bare, cracked, with broken toenails, and He's got jiggers.

Jesus has jiggers.

I have learned more about jiggers by now. They are fleas that burrow into the bare skin of people's feet.

These fleas latch onto blood cells and lay eggs, and within days they're a thousand times as big as when they entered. The eggs then hatch, mature, and lead to infestation, and the soles become itchy, red, and infected.

If jiggers remain untreated, the person is at risk of death.

Jesus has jiggers. But then, He's also all-encompassing and glorious.

This is the kingdom of heaven.

I think of Mother Teresa, who said, "I held the Host with two fingers and thought: How small Jesus made Himself, in order to show us that He doesn't expect great things of us, but rather little things with great love."[142]

His is a paradoxical kingdom. A kingdom of mustard seeds defeating mountains.

He looks at me now from His small place, and He says, *We do this for them, My daughter.*

The remnant of the nations will journey once a year to Jerusalem, Zechariah says, for the Feast of Tabernacles.[143] This Feast of Sukkot celebrates God's provision in the wilderness.

Lauren Winner describes Sukkot in her book *Girl Meets God*:

On Sukkot, Jewish families each build a hut, a sukkah, to remind themselves of the sukkot the Jews inhabited while they camped in the desert for forty years.... Rabbi Akiva, a Talmudic sage, says that the original sukkot were flimsy, ramshackle, twigs and bark and cactus needles [much like the shacks in Africa's slums, with their scraps of cardboard and aluminum], but another rabbi, Eliezar, says the sukkot were far grander—they were "clouds of glory" that accompanied the Jews all through their desert wanderings.... Today, the sukkah you would build might be an eight-foot cube, made from plywood held together with nails and twine. You cover the roof with greenery (the covering is called a *schach*, and it should be translucent enough to let in starlight) and invite neighborhood children to hang drawings on the walls. You eat all your meals in the sukkah,...and sometimes even sleep there.... It is while sitting in the sukkah that you learn lessons about dependence on God, that even the walls of your brick house are flimsy.[144]

In the slums, there's no forgetting God. They celebrate Sukkot all year round.

Yet Zechariah says there will be a day when "Holy to the Lord" will be written on all the bells of the horses. At the final Feast of Tabernacles, when the rich and the poor pick up their mats and walk to Jerusalem, the cooking pots will be like sacred bowls, "*and all who come to sacrifice…will cook in them.*"[145]

The ordinary made sacred. The sukkah made a cloud of glory.

And even as Treasure is rescued from the brink of death, a sort of anástasis, I hear the bells.

Oh, that we would press close to the dirt. Oh, that we would see the stars.

benediction

I have come to believe that there is more grace in becoming
wheat than there is in pulling up weeds.
—Michael Flynn[146]

2022 – EN ROUTE TO CANADA

There's a rustle of curtain, a silver trolley.

It's dinnertime on the plane. The stewardess tries to smile; she's a mother on a long trip with a hundred and fifty children.

"Chicken or fish?" she asks.

"Chicken," I say.

Plane life on a long flight has a rhythm, one I've come to know: doors closing, safety briefing, rolling along the tarmac, takeoff.

When the plane plateaus, the drinks roll out. Later, the meal comes, and finally the lights dim until they rise again like curtains revealing more drinks and a breakfast of sorts—usually some kind of European pastry—before the plane lands.

The man beside me is reading a nineteenth-century French book on Africa and its history entitled *La Femme*. He has silver hair and will later fall asleep, and he'll keep waking in fits, read another page, then, glasses slipping, fall back into dreams.

He's awake now, tray out; he opts for fish. *Bon appétit.* We smile at each other, a fellowship of sorts.

I bow over my food, say a simple prayer, unwrap the foil, resume watching *Babette's Feast.*

At this point in the film, the father, the dean of the community, has died; it's fifteen years later and an actual funeral has occurred to warrant the community's wearing black. Yet even after the funeral ends, the sisters, Martine and Philippa, continue to dress in dark clothing. Their brown shawls are now threadbare.

One rainy night, a stranger knocks on their door. The stranger is fearful, exhausted—a woman fleeing Paris and carrying a letter.

In the novel *Babette's Feast*, the author describes the woman as collapsing on their doorstep.

Will I recognize when God comes to me in a way I don't expect?

The letter the woman carries is from a former would-be suitor of Philippa's named Achille Papin, a man of class, an opera singer who, years earlier, had given Philippa singing lessons with the hopes of bringing her to the Paris stage. Philippa had taken a few lessons, but after Papin kissed her, she had requested her father to send him away.

The stranger, explains Papin, is Babette Hersant, whose husband and son have been killed in the civil war in France and whose own life is in danger. He asks if they will have mercy on her and take her in. Then he adds, almost as an aside, "Babette can cook."

When the sisters explain they cannot afford to pay her, Babette insists she will serve them with gratitude, without pay.

The sisters endeavor to be good examples of the Lutheran life for this poor Catholic woman.

They hope to eventually convert her.[147]

This is what I've learned these years of doing church: the gospel of God is the Bread of the Presence, and it reaches down into the deepest, darkest, ugliest recesses of the human spirit, the places polite chit-chat won't allow, the places watery juice doesn't open up, the places where crawfish and other creeping things of the swamps live.

These are the places in which we run to the altar and find the bread, still warm. Places in which we begin to get full. Where our only food becomes God Himself.

God is not peering in at us through stained-glass eyes. No, He's all flesh and tears and hugs on the boardwalk. He's with the men who are singing pub tunes and eating fish such as He served to the multitudes.

And when you find Him, He will pull you close and feed you until you feast until you laugh until you cannot help but pull others close too.

David feasted on holy bread. He danced with joy in his linen ephod as the ark of the Lord entered Jerusalem. And then he turned and fed the multitude gathered there—every man, every woman—a loaf of bread.[148]

The fed became the feeder. The broken became the fixer.

God is Spirit is Roaring Lion is the Very Source of Everything, and we should shake. Even as demons do.[149]

Yet this same God has donned an apron and is preparing us a banquet.

One with tumblers full of wine.

Part Three:

The Feeding

table

You have a God who hears you, the power of love behind you, the Holy Spirit within you, and all of heaven ahead of you. If you have the Shepherd, you have grace for every sin, direction for every turn, a candle for every corner, and an anchor for every storm. You have everything you need.
—Max Lucado[150]

2021 – KENYA

The hills look like *posho* here—like mounds of maize flour, water, and salt all lumped together.

We've arrived from Uganda, my team and I, after multiple breakdowns of our vehicle and delays at the border. We've spent hours on the road, passing storefronts of all colors advertising condoms and fruit drinks and "Zam Zam Restaurant." We've passed muscular men riding bikes bearing heavy loads of sticks strapped

table 149

to a thin rim on the back tire. We've seen women and children in rice fields, bent over and swatting bugs.

Finally, across the border, we've met Pastor John. His long, brown face always seems to be smiling. He's wearing an oversized leather jacket and baggy trousers, and he greets us with "Jambo, jambo, my brothers and sister!"

We drive now through the hills of Kenya into Funyula, into the land of Yellowwood and Moringa trees. We stop at four mud churches where children in baggy T-shirts stare at us and pastors and elders greet us, and then we carry on to John's home. It's near evening, and the cicadas are singing.

John calls his wife, Layla, his "lollipop." She's in the outdoor kitchen but comes, shy, to meet us, laughing behind a small hand. Her form is petite, and she is pretty and young for having seven children. She doesn't speak much English, just keeps laughing and gesturing toward the small clay hut that serves as their living room.

John first shows us our rooms—I'm in one hut, and they've somehow dragged a four-poster bed in for me, along with a mosquito net. I can't exclaim enough, and John's smile only gets bigger.

I drop off my bags, and we head out again.

Next to the main house is an outdoor kitchen constructed mostly from iron sheets, with an orange plywood door. Behind that, a piggery. Laundry clings to the bushes and grass, drying; piles of red bricks sit stacked, and children are everywhere—fourteen in total, seven of them adopted. They stare at me with saucer-eyes; some giggle, others touch my skin. A few come and shake our hands, bow.

We sit on couches in the hut that is their dining room, a curtain dividing it from John and Layla's bedroom. The door is ajar, and chickens and cats wander in and out. The printer and laptop we helped John purchase are covered by bedsheets to protect them from the dust. A basin and a pitcher are brought, and a young girl pours water over our hands.

Food is spread on the white cloth covering the small coffee table, and John stands in the doorway, his shadow tall. He thanks God for the meal.

I think of Elijah, fed by the widow at Zarephath.[151] How the flour and oil didn't run out because she believed.

It's my first time eating *posho*, or *ugali*. It's Kenya's bread, and my hands sink into the warm dough. I pull at it, pile it onto my plate, add fish sauce, rice, beans, and greens. I've got a mound of food, and I use the *posho* as my spoon, scooping up the greens and the beans with the dough.

For dessert, it's pineapple and mango and avocado, all sweet and sticky in my mouth, and my stomach is full, the *posho* like a pillow beneath my ribs. I could sleep.

Suddenly a man enters, disheveled and sweaty. He greets us, smooths out his shirt, asks John if they can talk. They step outside, and we hear voices, and then John returns.

"This man is one of my elders," he says, "and his wife somehow thought you were coming to her house for supper. So she cooked a great feast, even killing a goat, and now it sits. But I told them you've already eaten, and you've traveled so far, so you must rest."

I look at my team of tired men from Uganda. I'm picturing this woman weeping into her apron. Cooking all day. Now with no guests.

"How can we not go?" I whisper to the team. They nod. The *posho* sits heavy.

"Pastor John, we must go," I tell him.

So he calls a taxi, and we climb in, some of the men curling up in the trunk so we can all fit. Then we begin the long drive to the elder's house. Miles and miles of bumpy red road, with us squished

table 151

together. We begin to sing, our hymns rising, then we grow quiet again as the journey stretches. All the while I pray, "God, make me hungry again."

By the time we arrive, it is pitch-black. A group has gathered, and they call us over to a clay and brick home filled with light. We are met by the arms of a beaming woman, the elder's wife, and there, on the table, another feast.

More *posho*, more rice and beans and greens; and the family goat, sacrificed for us. We take a little of each dish, but they keep pushing us to eat more until the food is too much. We're fuller than full and might never hunger again.

Fed by those who hunger. And us thinking we are the ones doing the feeding. With our split cod and ale-and-bread soup.

Candle wax drips, pooling in the corners of the clay house, and we sigh a sleepy sigh. Stretch our legs.

Men enter then, carrying a girl. She looks dead. She's maybe fifteen, stretched out flat as a board. They lay her on the dirt floor. Air puffs from her pursed lips, and her eyes remain open, unblinking, as though in a trance. My own eyes begin to water. If only she could blink.

She's demon-possessed, they say. She normally stands all day, staring at the wall, unmoving. A cult pastor cursed her, they say, when she left his church.

They begin to yell at God in spiritual tongues, punching the air; others gather around, place hands on her, pray with increasing volume, as though one can scare the demons away. She keeps staring at nothing. I put my hand on her hand. Her skin is cold. I try to listen, try to pray. After half an hour, she relaxes a little, sits up, blinks. They say it's a start. They say there are a lot of demons.

My team begins to leave, so I gather my things, step into the black shawl of night. But something pulls me back into the house of candles.

I duck in, see pastors trying to push the girl into a chair, but her legs won't bend. Her face looks so tired. Wrung out like a tattered cloth.

And Jesus is here with this girl, as He was with me in the hospital bed, as He was with Jairus's daughter.[152]

And He speaks over her now, as He spoke over the deep at creation's birth, over the Red Sea when it split in two, over the wind and the waves to still the gale.

He speaks over her through me. "Rest," I say.

I put my hand on this girl's shoulder.

Her eyes find mine, lock hold.

"Rest," I say again.

Her knees buckle; she sinks into the chair.

"Rest, dear daughter," I say a final time.

Tears fill her eyes, and I hug her. Kiss her head.

Rest is the ancient position of one who feasts. It's a reclining, a lying down, a surrender to the table.

Jesus reclined at the table with Lazarus.[153] He reclined at the table with His disciples.[154] And He reclines with us.

"*Here I am!*" He says to the church. "*I stand at the door and knock. If anyone hears my voice and opens the door, I will come in and eat with that person, and they with me.*"[155]

First, to hear His voice.

Then, to open the door wide, to choose the better thing.[156]

This One who is the feast.

bread

Your Master has taken the bread and has blessed and broken it, and then He has given it to you. Is that the end of the process? Do you stand there and munch your own personal morsel with a miserable self-satisfaction? No, if you are, indeed, disciples of Christ, you will…break, then, your bread among the hungry that surround you!
—Charles H. Spurgeon[157]

2018 – UGANDA

The fish eye is so big it's like the eye of God.

It peers up from the plate, this cichlid. I'm sure it blinks.

It's close to Christmas. My family has come with our team to Uganda to feast with our friends.

The kids pick at the tomatoes and fried potatoes. My younger son holds his head in his hands. My older son swallows. My daughter, who's only three, tells me the fish eye is scary.

Trent emerges from Lake Victoria. The Ugandans around us stare at my dripping-wet husband. Swimming isn't common here. He sits on the beach with us in his wet shorts, thanks God, dives into the googly-eyed fish.

I think of Jesus cooking for His friends on the beach. How He catches the fish, I don't know. How He forgives them, I don't know.

The disciples just up and leave Jesus in His newly risen glory, return to their old life. Like three years of miracles and being nailed to the cross mean nothing.

They spend all night fishing, catch nothing, and then Jesus shows up on the beach. Lights a fire and cooks them breakfast. Suggests they try throwing the net on the other side of the boat.

The net immediately fills; they lug it to shore, and He feeds them. Again.

Then He chooses them. Again.

He says, *"Feed my sheep."*

He says it again and again.

He talks about Peter being led places he won't want to go.[158]

Later, He leaves, disappears into the sky.[159] He reappears as holy flames atop His followers' heads,[160] and the disciples finally get it. They set the world on fire.

We're renting a guesthouse where our family can all stay together. Because it's Christmastime, our Ugandan team drags in a wide green bush and sticks balloons on it. We eat and drink and pray together. Their kids play with our kids. Balloons are a global language. My younger son kicks a soccer ball with one of the "uncles," while my older son builds a brick house with one of the other boys, and my daughter is held by aunties who coo over her blond pigtails.

We eat coconut and jackfruit and pawpaw and drink thick mango juice. The ends of our fingers smell like orange peel. When we lie on white sheets at night, our bodies leave red dust prints behind.

We visit the school and the dorms where the teenage mothers stay. Trent and the boys play catch with village children who laugh behind their hands.

Hundreds of elderly women, and some men, gather for a *jajja* outreach at the school compound. They gather under white tents in plastic chairs, all bent and smiling, their eyes like shiny pebbles in a dry riverbed.

We sing with them and kiss their gnarled fingers. Some of them have walked here without shoes. They eat from plates piled high with rice and beans and *matoke*. They go home with packages of rice and flour and sugar and salt and soap.

One afternoon we slip away to the Nile River. There, I get baptized again. This time by immersion.

I want every part of me clean. I want to run with the Samaritan woman, the rivers rushing inside me.

We take a boat to a shallow part of the river. I stand in the waters of the same river in which Moses floated in Egypt. A Ugandan pastor goes through the baptismal words with me: "I will rise up with Him, from today."

I go under, emerge. There's no dove, no heavenly ovation. Just my daughter in her life jacket, sitting on a rock, begging her dad to hold her, and the splash of my younger son jumping into the river. Doing his own baptism.

But I feel the water everywhere. I feel it washing me.

The pastor prays, asking God to make rivers flow from my belly. "That so many nations will drink out of her," he says. "May the Spirit of God flow through her to the thirsty nations."

I climb into the boat, dripping.

The director hands me a new outfit she's purchased from one of the many vendors using her own money. It seems significant. Like I'm putting on new skin.

I have no idea she has been stealing from us.

I have no idea our director has been lying to the teenage mothers, saying I don't want them to eat, that she's been using the funds sent to feed them to line her own pockets instead. To start her own shop. I have no idea that she bribes them not to say anything when I come.

This same woman whose son played with my son, whose daughter shared clothes with my daughter, who gave me her bed when I came to visit, who rode a *boda boda* each day to the slums, sometimes in the rain; who met day after day with women in a tin-roofed shack to sing and pray and give them their stipends, who helped us start a training center, who helped us start Lulu.

This woman found the money bag.

It's as if she kissed Jesus and sold Him for silver.[161]

"We must offer ourselves to God by saying, 'Lord…let me be grist to your mill and make me into a hard grain so that I will make good flour,'" says Catherine Doherty in *Apostolic Farming*. "An apostolic farmer makes of himself bread, so as to feed others, even as he is fed daily on the Eternal Bread—the wheat for which he has grown himself."[162]

The red dirt takes a long time to wash from our feet.

Leonard Ravenhill says, "If you want to be like Jesus, remember, He had a wilderness, a Gethsemane and a Judas."[163]

I now have a Judas.

I learn of the director's betrayal after coming home.

The house of sod crumbles.

The red finally washes off. It looks like watery blood.

It's been said some indigenous peoples used to bury fish beneath their crop plants.[164] From the dying of these fish, wheat grew, which was then ground into flour, then kneaded into bread.

The church was built on the backs of fishermen.

Fishermen who were martyred, one of them crucified upside down. Buried, that we might grow.

A year before the betrayal, I stood on Mount Sugar Loaf, the crumbling red dust of a collapsed hill in Sierra Leone.

I stood where hundreds of bodies lay. Beneath me were buried homes, crushed four months earlier by a torrential mudslide.

I stood where onlookers had gathered on flat roofs in the middle of the night as the mountain and houses and pathways and bikes and cars all slid, as mothers still gripping babies were washed away.

I stood where an all-night prayer vigil had taken place, a vigil in a church on the hill, crushed by the mud and rain. None of the congregation had survived. All of them taken, mid-prayer.

I stood where others had fallen.

Some things can only be wept. My limbs shook as I walked across the red rubble of yesterday's homes, yesterday's laughter, yesterday's children, and I cried out to a God who didn't make sense.

I thought of those mothers, clinging to their babies.

I thought of the prostrate faithful, the pastor and his wife and his family, the praises and confessions in the midnight hour in that little church, then the rumblings of the earth beneath them, the burial.

Jesus loved Mary and Martha and Lazarus, and so He stayed away for two extra days. Because He loved them, He waited. Their brother's body rotting four days in the tomb. When Jesus finally arrived, He didn't apologize, just asked if they believed.[165]

Jesus's sweat, like blood, on His skin. The cross digging into His torn shoulders as He climbed Calvary. A hill that would crumble and shake, the wrath of God ripping up the ground and the graves and the temple cloth.

Red water running from His side.

No one understanding. Could this be the King? This defeated man, this impoverished, shattered man on a cross?

Like a fish buried.

Then the hills filled with life, like lungs inhaling, and they exhaled Lazarus, they exhaled Jesus Christ.

"Take off the grave clothes and let him go," Jesus said.[166]

"He is not here; he has risen!" the angels said.[167]

All I saw was death. I stood on mass graves.

All I saw was the tomb where Lazarus lay. The cross where Jesus died.

But there was a resurrection happening even now. There was a crop rising from the ground where the fish were buried. Wheat for the world.

There is an eternal prayer vigil taking place in heaven with hundreds of Sierra Leonean worshippers who will never go hungry again, who will never thirst again, who will never cry again. There are mothers holding babies who are laughing and singing, mothers who will never lose their children again.

We cannot see the blessing. We can only see the casket.

But from the soil, He will receive back the seed.

I turned to walk down the hill. An old man watched me from a distance, seated on a broken plastic chair.

How much had he seen? How much had he lost?

I nodded at him. He nodded at me.

As we enter into life with one another, God comes alive. The church—the one we'd thought had crumbled—rises.

In *Crazy Love*, Francis Chan says God measures our lives by how much we love. "We are loaded down with too many good things, more than we could ever need, while others are desperate for a small loaf," he writes.[168]

For better or worse, this loving the world is like a marriage. The husband feeding the wife, and the wife feeding the husband, and their becoming one flesh over many years of making mistakes and starting over. Like the church. Like the kneading of dough.

We have parted ways with the old director and are starting over. Some pastors have left, loyal to the director.

Pastor Solomon, with his huge smile, chooses to stay.

Solomon is poor, but he laughs like he's not. He's small and wiry, his smile spilling out of his eyes. When he sees me he grips my hands in his, stumbles over his English words. Behind him is a string of children, clinging to his gentleness. He was the first to recruit teenage mothers for our free school. He walked for miles to bring them to us. His church follows him much the same way the children do.

Solomon reminds me of the hope that is "the thing with feathers," as Emily Dickinson calls it, the thing that sings an endless, wordless tune:

> I've heard it in the chillest land,
> And on the strangest sea;
> Yet, never, in extremity,
> It asked a crumb of me.[169]

Oswald Chambers says, "Song birds are taught to sing in the dark."[170]

It's night for my soul right now. The refrain has been lost.

Solomon is teaching me to sing again. And never does he ask a crumb of us, so we offer one to him. We offer him a bicycle.

His smile spills white. He researches the cost of a bike with good tires and a good seat, one that will help him travel the many miles between church and home. Then he tells us the cost, and we send the money. A little while later we meet up with him again. He brings the bike. But the seat is torn and the bike a bit rusty.

Turns out he'd met a woman in desperate need, had given some of the bike funds to her. So he couldn't get the bike he'd been wanting.

"But this one will do just fine, thank you, thank you!" He can't stop shaking our hands.

He'd shared the little he had.

Solomon's refrain is one of praise. He flies it like a yellow kite over the villages. Despite the weeping of earth and man, Solomon smiles as he pedals.

He's learned how to sing in the dark.

And it's because of people like him that I press on. Even in Canada, I can hear him singing.

Our faith is much like yeast. It grows better in the shadows.

In the warm, wet flesh of the dough, in the tomblike place where no light can shine, yeast grows.

Yeast is saprophytic. Direct sunlight hurts it. Instead, it breaks down dead organic-carbon sources in the dark and feeds off those.

Like resurrection. A rescue of dead cells.

Death is no longer scary to me. Not like when Grandma Amelia died. Now I know it happens every day. Death peels away everything that isn't important, like the skin of the fruit.

But I don't want to die, and it feels like I am.

Physically. My body feels like death.

I go to doctor after doctor. I can't eat or sleep due to the pain. It goes on for months. Antibiotics don't help, neither do probiotics or pain meds. Finally I learn that our former director, the one we let go, the one who betrayed us, has been attending a "church" where they learn how to curse people.

And much like the cult pastor who cursed the girl in Kenya, this woman has been cursing me.

The women who are still in touch with her whisper to me: they tell me terrible things—that this director has even taken a little box and put a doll in it and buried it in the ground, saying the doll was me, and commanding the doll to die.

I begin to pray. Because I've been resurrected before. And "*a curse without cause shall not alight,*"[171] I remind the Lord, and the pain begins to leave. But oh, the breaking. The continuous kneeling and trusting, but sometimes the screaming and the kicking and the flailing: "Why, God? Why, when I've given You everything?"

Brother Lawrence would have told me to rest in God's love.

He would have told me that "thinking often spoils everything and that evil usually begins with our thoughts."[172]

I would have pouted, then agreed.

After all, who can disagree with a lame monk who makes even washing dishes holy?

Brother Lawrence saw all of us as trees in winter, with little to give, stripped of leaves and color and growth, whom God loves unconditionally anyway.[173]

But have you ever seen a barren tree covered in hoarfrost? It's as if all of heaven's glory chooses those sad, faithful trees. And one morning as you're driving to church, you see their bony arms wrapped in white satin and jewels. Like row after row of ladies-in-waiting.

So I rest in this unconditional love. Because I am that barren tree. I have nothing left to give. I just reach up and wait for Him to cover me.

Let the songs and the yeast grow. I'm feasting on love in the presence of my enemies.

After all, nothing stays dead around God.

The showbread in the temple was not round and plump.

It may have been shaped like a "dancing ship"—with a narrow hull, the sides pointing up, much like a V-shape. Two stacks of six loaves were placed before the Lord for seven days. And every Shabbat, those twelve loaves were replaced by twelve fresh ones. Yet somehow the old ones never grew moldy or stale. Some say it was because of a special recipe. I say it was because they were in the presence of God.

Jewish tradition tells us that when the children of Israel made the pilgrimage to the temple three times a year—for Passover, Shavuot, and Sukkot—they were able to view the showbread. And the priest would point to the bread and say, "Look at how beloved you are by G-d!"[174]

The showbread isn't always warm though.

Sometimes it's cracked and bloody and nailed to a cross.

Communion means union with, fellowship with, the sufferings of Christ.

The Eucharist is God pointing to His Son on the cross and saying, "Look at how beloved you are!"

Will we partake?

The Korean War orphaned a country. More than a hundred thousand children were robbed of parents, homes, and security. Relief agencies flooded the scene and began to care for these homeless ones. But they found that even though the children were receiving three meals a day, they were struggling to sleep, filled with anxiety and fear. When asked what they were afraid of, the children said they were worried they wouldn't be fed the next day.

And so nurses in one orphanage began to tuck a single piece of bread into the hands of each child at bedtime. A security blanket of sorts, assuring the child that he or she would, in fact, be fed upon waking.[175]

I too am falling asleep clinging to bread, to my God, even as I fear tomorrow. Jesus is my safety, my comfort, my peace, my food, my drink, my bedtime Shema. And I whisper as I weep, "Hear O Israel: The Lord our God, the Lord is One."[176]

And even as I cry out to Yahweh in the black folds of night, the bread crusty and crumbling in my warm palm, a kind of kibbutz happens.

The Jewish kibbutz is the concept of a small agrarian community that works together to transform a desert area in Israel, the cultivation of an arid place. Adopting once infertile plots of land, these cooperatives have succeeded in bringing water, life, and food to impossible places.

It's the living picture of Isaiah 35. Everything in the kibbutz is sustainable and sustaining, and the hymn of the wilderness resounds and responds. As Isaiah rejoiced:

> *Even the wilderness and desert will be glad in those days.*
>   *The wasteland will rejoice and blossom with spring crocuses.*
> *Yes, there will be an abundance of flowers*
>   *and singing and joy!*
> *The deserts will become as green as the mountains of Lebanon,*
>   *as lovely as Mount Carmel or the plain of Sharon.*
> *There the Lord will display his glory,*
>   *the splendor of our God.*[177]

And I see it, even as I cling to the crust. I hold Jesus in my sweaty palm, yet He slips out of my grasp and fills the whole world. He transforms the wasteland, filling it with His glory, pouring out salve and planting flowers, and everywhere springs burst up, filled with life, resplendent. Glory.

Miremba comes to help us in Uganda. And she, along with my friend Emmanuel, transforms the arid landscape of Uganda into a home of hope for the world to take refuge in.

Slowly my grip on the crust loosens as I realize the Bread Himself is actually holding me.

wine

Since we took a bite out of the fruit and tore into our own
souls, that drain hole where joy seeps away,
God's had this wild secretive plan. He means to fill us with
glory again. With glory and grace.
—Ann Voskamp[178]

2018 – SOUTH SUDAN

He was born beneath a shea tree.

His mother gave birth to him one night while she was out gathering sticks. She just lay down in the forest and labored on the moss, as one does, no doubt biting on a piece of twig.

And Muneeb came out, bloody and screaming, into a world that was bloody and screaming. He was born in Sudan, a country ravaged by civil war. And in 1990, at age seventeen, Muneeb ran. He ran from all the dying. He reached the Nile, the river dividing South Sudan from Uganda, the army hard on his heels. The soldiers were "beating people, raping women, taking their property," Muneeb relates. He had no way across the river.

But God made a way. He made a footbridge. He pressed floating leaves together, Muneeb says, and a path formed, and Muneeb walked across the water on the bridge made of leaves. When the army reached the river, God scattered the bridge.

"That was the time I began to have feelings about God," he declares. "I knew He could protect His people."

Months earlier God had whispered "South Sudan" to me, but civil war still raged, and we didn't know anyone there. So we fasted and prayed for forty days for the Lord to confirm He indeed wanted us there, and for God to raise up someone for us to partner with.

On the final day of the fast, I'm standing in the airport in Uganda, waiting to head home. I hear the sputter of the air conditioner, smell the salty skin of a hundred travelers. I'm so tired it feels like my bones are weeping.

In front of me stands a man talking on his phone—an African man whose profile seems familiar. He's wearing a hat with a Christian slogan and a T-shirt with the name of a humanitarian organization.

I look at his bag, see his name in black script: it's the very man who first led me to Uganda four years earlier. And he's standing right in front of me.

I tap his arm. He turns. "Emily?" he says, nearly drops his phone. Later we talk in the waiting area. He's just returned from— of all places—the South Sudanese refugee camps.

He tells me terrible things: eleven thousand children have been turned into soldiers and child brides; 1.4 million South Sudanese live in camps in deplorable conditions, and 84 percent of them are women and youth.

I realize the miracles are not behind me. They're never actually behind us. They're only ever just a prayer away.

For forty days we've been fasting and praying for South Sudan. Today is the last day of the fast. And God has made a footbridge.

My leader turns to me then and says, "Will you help them?"

I don't have to think.

"Yes," I tell him. "We will."

We select three men from our Ugandan team. It's our first faith mission. They go in prayer, led by the Lord through visions and dreams. They go to find someone we can work with. It takes three months, but they find him. It is Muneeb.

Muneeb wears a leather cowboy hat. He's a long hugger and a close talker, and he unites the tribes under him. He's a pastor with a vision who started a tailoring school for mothers and a preschool for their children. And he takes in youth from child-headed homes.

Child-headed homes are grass huts, dotting the camps, holding only children. These homes are like grass-covered wombs, and beside them are often dirt mounds where the children have been forced to bury their parents.

These young ones live on a cup of rice a day as they stare at the horizon, waiting for hope to appear.

I'm reminded of Elisabeth Elliot and her book *These Strange Ashes*. In it she shares a parable about Jesus and His disciples.

A story is told of Jesus and His disciples walking one day along a stony road. Jesus asked each of them to choose a stone to carry for Him. John, it is said, chose a large one while Peter chose the smaller. Jesus led them then to the top of a mountain and commanded that the stones be made bread. Each disciple, by this time tired and hungry, was allowed to eat the bread he held in his hand, but of course Peter's was not sufficient to satisfy his hunger. John gave him some of his.

Some time later Jesus again asked the disciples to pick up a stone to carry. This time Peter chose the largest of all. Taking them to a river, Jesus told them to cast the stones into the water. They did so, but looked at one another in bewilderment.

"For whom," asked Jesus, "did you carry the stone?"[179]

I'm Jacob, wrestling with God.

Who am I carrying this ministry for?

What if, in the end, I have nothing to show?

Will I still do it for Him?

He tells me to cast the stone into the river.

Even the smallest stone leaves a ripple.

The time comes to send funds by wire.

We don't have money for South Sudan. We're short $1,500.

I fall on my face beside the washer, feel the rumble and swish of the machine's stomach.

And I pray.

My prayers are like sighs right now, deep, suffering sighs, falling onto the chest of the Trinity. I hear *Be still* and *I'm pleased with you* even as I struggle to believe we're actually supposed to walk on water. I remind God we've banked all our hope on Him.

I wake the next morning in perfect peace.

Midday, I get a message.

It's from our treasurer, saying a partner has just called her. God had told this partner that The Lulu Tree was experiencing a shortage. He wanted to know how much we were short so he could supply it.

No one had told this partner of the need. No one had posted it on our blog or shared about it on social media. Jehovah Jireh alone had posted it on this person's heart.

I have nothing but praise within me. I go into my bedroom, close the door, kneel down and worship.

He's here in this hiding place, in this pulpy place of branch meeting vine.

Brother Lawrence says he can't do big things for God, so he just focuses on doing little things.[180]

My little thing is to cling to the vine.

Children are God's little things.

He loves them with a great love. Like Razia, the girl who hid so long she forgot her name.

Muneeb's friend Jamal lives in South Sudan, in Nimule—a city of sixty-four tribes. He's a pastor who also loves children.

He tells us about Razia, and we cry.

The sun was the color of blood orange that day. Razia could hear the skitter of chickens and the clearing of a rooster's throat.

The swish of mothers' skirts, the snapping of branches, and the crackling of fires.

Her baba and umi rose from their mats, smiled at her. Umi kissed her cheek. Then her parents rolled up their mats, stepped into the sun: Umi, to collect water, and Baba, to gather firewood. Razia's job was to sweep the house and put things in order.

They never came back.

Soldiers had ambushed them.

Screams, then silence.

The silence was loud, like a whoosh, like trees falling.

In Africa, trees tell a child where he lives. The sound of the birds singing in the trees, the colors of the seasonal fruit they gather for breakfast. So when trees are cut down, children don't know where they live anymore.

The birds stopped singing the day Razia's parents died.

It had been four years since that horrible day. She hadn't left her house since. She was still putting it in order. No one knew her except her neighbors, who sometimes slipped her bowls of rice.

Then Pastor Jamal came.

He was tall, and he ducked low, entered her tiny home. She cowered against the wall.

"I'm not going to hurt you, friend," he said. His voice was as soft as the night sky. "I'm here to help. What's your name?"

He crouched low on the dirt floor.

What was her name? She tried to remember. It had been so long. She recalled Umi—her gentle smile, her arms outstretched—saying, "Razia, sweetheart, come eat."

It had been so long.

"Razia," she said. "My name is Razia."

The birds sang the day Jamal took Razia home.

He took her to his church compound, where widows and teenage mothers cooked and cleaned and laughed together.

Every week the mothers spread blankets beneath a leafy tamarind tree to count their microloan money.

And every week the teenage mothers went to school.

Razia went with them.

Everywhere, trees are planted on Jamal's compound. Guarded by little fences.

One day these trees will hold birds and fruit. One day they will tell the children where they live.

I am a branch. I try to tape myself to the Vine, but I keep falling off.

"I knew full well that there was in the root, the stem, abundant fatness," says Hudson Taylor, "but how to get it into my puny little branch was the question."[181]

I walk the streets of my Canadian Dutch hamlet, praying, trying to believe—in spite of the snow and the cold and the quiet—that God hears me. That God not only hears but answers, that He moves hearts and minds because of my words. Because of my faith.

I sound like I have faith, but deep down, I do not. Like Taylor, I keep doubting, again and again.

Afraid of being hurt again. The tape isn't sticky enough.

The Lulu Tree, the shea tree, or vitellaria, originates in South Sudan. As with the grapevine, or vitis, Lulu's fruit is not sudden. Shea nuts take years to mature.

Grapes take months. Grapes are born from shoots that stem from buds from the previous year. Winter is the test of their endurance.

It's a test for me too.

Will I keep believing God loves me?

Will I trust Him in spite of the betrayal?

Will I keep loving His people?

Will my heart stay soft?

The buds that harden over winter are pruned off, making room for tender ones.

Then there are the flowers, which are small. Much like the people God uses to do His big works. On my desk, I have another quote by Taylor, written by my mum in blue ink with her tiny handwriting on a faded recipe card:

> God chose me because I was weak enough. God does not do His great works by large committees. He trains somebody to be quiet enough, and little enough, and then He uses him.[182]

The flowers fall to make room for the fruit—grapes that are big and round and bursting with magenta-colored juice. The animals come and eat the berries, and this is how the seeds are spread. In the crushing. Much like how wine is made. Or how shea-nut oil is produced from the crushing of nuts.

Nothing good comes easy.

Except faith.

Faith is what I learn on my lonely prayer vigils. Faith, God shows me, is easy. Because it's a resting, a heaving of myself upon Him, and it's He who holds me fast. This Jesus, who is the faithful One.

Taylor teaches me this too, writing:

> I saw not only that Jesus will never leave me, but that I am a member of His body, of His flesh and of His bones. The vine is not the root merely, but *all*—root, stem, branches, twigs, leaves, flowers, fruit. And Jesus is not that alone—He is soil and sunshine, air and showers, and ten thousand times more than we have ever dreamed, wished for or needed.[183]

And so prayer becomes a Eucharist. A meal of thankfulness. A falling on my face in the presence of a mighty King, pure worship, and agreement with His plans for His world.

2018 – LIBERIA

The dark becomes a comfortable thing again, much like the cupped space between two hands, a space big enough for a bird. A thing with feathers.

And Jesus takes my hand and whispers, *Liberia*.

So we fast for forty days for this country that clings to the left hip of Africa.

Liberia, or "Land of Freedom," was founded in 1822 by freeborn and newly freed African Americans. Over half of them died before the country gained independence from America. It's a land of turmoil and mistrust, of rough roads and rougher people.

Africa is all out in the open, nothing to hide. There's no guessing. Africa has no reason to go inside except to sleep. And sometimes, people even sleep under the stars. And so you get both the good and the ugly together. Life and death walk hand in hand. And God is incarnate there. He is talked to and walked with and sung about by people, whether they are pulling up roots or bathing babies in basins or clipping clothes to the line.

And when we launch a second faith mission into Liberia, we send Pastor Ibrahim of Sierra Leone with just a map and a prayer. He has no idea where he's going, but he's got God to take him there. First, he goes to Monrovia, where he knows someone who helps orphans. He thinks this might be the person to help us with our work. But God says no, and in a dream he's shown where to go.

So Ibrahim moves north, journeying along winding red roads, to a little town called Zorzor. The Bethlehem of Liberia. God takes him to the door of a church woman. And there, in her house, lives a man named Victor. He and his family live there because they can't afford their own home. And this, God says, is the one He has chosen.

Ibrahim says, "You're the one," then starts the long trek home to Sierra Leone, leaving Victor to wonder.

And over the years, we grow to love Pastor Victor and his wife and their many children. We help them buy goats and raise pigs and plant a nursery of palm and coconut trees. Victor sends videos of them chopping down a forest to clear land to grow rice, because everything is jungle in Liberia. And the community women gather and sing and pull up roots.

When I go to Liberia, I shake the women's hands, and they nod and keep on singing as they plant rice. The rice grows. Later we receive another video of them harvesting the rice, with more singing.

And Victor feeds the rice to the five hundred children who attend his school.

He'd come to Zorzor with nothing. Just a Bible in his pocket. Now he oversees seventy-five churches.

As a boy, Victor was unloved by his father. He was the only child in his family who didn't get Christmas presents or school fees. They called him "Chicken Feet" because he had no shoes. One day, at fourteen, he ran away to school. And he made a promise to God that, one day, he would start a school for kids like him. For kids who didn't belong.

In 2023, we attend his high school's graduation. I speak to the students under a canopy of palms. I tell them about Victor, how he came here with nothing, not even five stones, how he fought the giant of doubt anyway and won. Because faith is easy when it's a gift.

We stay in Victor's home, and Ibrahim can't stop telling me, "Oh, thank you, ma'am, thank you, for building him a home."

It's a small zinc castle, painted white, and we sit on plastic chairs and eat roasted plantain, all orange and buttery, and Victor laughs. Long and hard. Like a child who is loved.

2021 – GUINEA

Again, God whispers.

He says, *Guinea*—a nation in West Africa, formerly a territory of France. We fast and pray, then send Ibrahim again, with Victor from Liberia, to find the one God has chosen to lead Lulu in Guinea. Another mission.

Together they walk with God during the long trip to Mamou, the town where God tells them to go. They travel through countless checkpoints. They trek through rain. Ibrahim gets sick with malaria and typhoid, but still they journey to where no church can be seen and even the Muslim call to prayer sounds scared.

Eventually, they meet Pastor Augustin. Ibrahim says that as soon as he saw him, he felt peace.

When I finally go to Guinea in 2023, that peace holds me— even as I'm threatened with jail for taking a photo at a checkpoint.

They interrogate us for hours. Finally Augustin says I'm his spiritual daughter, he's named his daughter after me, and they would be disgracing him by putting me in jail.

So the police demand money instead. Which is all they really wanted in the first place.

We drive deep into Guinea, past the bleak faces of a dozen mosques, to a two-room home. Augustin's wife is seated outside at a charcoal fire. His daughter, a baby, is held by a young girl.

They wrap us in hugs, we stumble over language, and we eat together. Rice and chicken, the juices dripping down our fingers. There's a hole in the ground for a toilet. Augustin's wife boils us hot water for a bath over her little charcoal fire.

They give me their room.

That night Augustin doesn't sleep, for fear Muslims will burn our vehicle.

"Any new converts, I tell them to keep wearing their hijab, to keep going to the mosque, until they're ready to die," he says. "Then they can leave."

The next day is a Bible school graduation in a tiny church strung with streamers. We gather with thirty-five men and women who've passed the theological courses, and we eat more chicken and rice, and we dance together. A big man sitting in the back bellows out songs. Drums beat and feet stamp and hands clap.

Our car breaks down as we leave Guinea. We pull into a garage.

A woman sits in a colorful dress, feet outstretched, surrounded by spilled diesel and old tires.

A young boy in cutoff pants hands tools to the only mechanic, who bangs on things in the engine. The sun pulses, a red blister.

Other boys in rags gather around the hood.

Another boy runs past us. He stops, turns to look at me, grins. Then he races to catch up with a friend who's kicking a ball.

The call to prayer crackles.

"Jésus vous aime," I tell the boys when we leave. "Jesus loves you." Light breaks across their faces. Their hands wave like brown flags.

And I see the little things.

Giving way to God.

mangoes

Don't desire happiness, for its staying power is weak.
Don't even desire joy itself, but instead desire Him who is joy.
Desire Him, long for Him, yearn for Him.
When you have found Him, delight in Him and He will give
you the desires of your heart.
—Sherwood E. Wirt[184]

2020 – CANADA

Funny, the places we go, when we don't go anywhere at all.

The water pipes creak like bones in the cold. Everyone is hushed in sleep except me, here, before the burning bush of my woodstove. And in prayer, I hear, *You won't be traveling this year.*

I don't understand, but I scribble it in my journal. Tell my board. Ask them to pray for confirmation.

A few weeks later, Trent comes home from work, tells me about a pandemic. I listen with half an ear, as I do to much of the news.

Two weeks later, Trent tells me it's gone global. This COVID-19 with its terrible cough and its many masks.

Piano lessons and schools and church buildings are shut down. People rush to purchase toilet paper and guns. Fear leads to confusion leads to conspiracy and hostility, and I contract shingles.

In the midst of it all, God tells me He is incubating His people. He is fulfilling the cry of His Son:

Jerusalem, Jerusalem, you who kill the prophets and stone those sent to you, how often I have longed to gather your children together, as a hen gathers her chicks under her wings, and you were not willing.[185]

I know about incubation. We grow chicks in an ancient incubator, the kind you need to rotate by hand.

For twenty-one days, three times a day, Trent rotates the eggs to make sure the embryos don't die. It is now three weeks into the cycle. At night we all crouch over the aluminum lid. Trent opens it. The air smells like warm, wet grass. A bowl of water keeps the eggs soft.

And when we lift a candle to each egg, looking for life, we gasp over glimpses of veins and wings and beaks, much like the image of a baby in an ultrasound.

The rotating has stopped, and a faint chirping sounds. A newly hatched chick sings—brave, alone—and then, from surrounding eggs, rises a chorus of tiny chick voices, greeting him, even as they peck at their shells.

The one who's escaped first sings for the others. A song of freedom. "One day, you too will be free," he carols.

Sometimes a chick is almost free, but not quite, and so on it struggles. How I want to help! But any interference will hurt the bird—can even kill it. The relentless pecking at its shell is necessary for its survival, a strengthening of muscle and resolve.

And when they're finally free, how quickly the chicks eat and drink and trip over their feet and become big and feathered.

And then, just when we think they won't ever—they do. These same ones who were once eggs, produce eggs: some blue, some brown, some green. Some double-yolkers, some that seem half-baked, with a wobbly, transparent shell.

Beyond the coop, though, the world seems to have stopped. Again, the Spirit whispers, *Incubation*.

And even as the weeks pass, we feel the hand of the Father tenderly rotating His church, looking for signs of life. Delighting over glimpses of charity and kindness and faith.

And then, the rotating stops. As if God leaves.

It's our turn now.

It's our turn to do the hard work. To peck away at our shells. To seek Him. So we begin to chip at the hardness of our hearts, at the walls, at the fears. And even as the shell persists and we begin to faint, we hear the gentle voice of the Father, singing. Because He hasn't left—He's simply been waiting. He sings to His people, "One day, you too will be free." And from deep within the saddest and hardest places, the greatest longings, the deepest fears, a song emerges in response. His people stir—new life forming somehow out of the seeming impossible.

From within eggs that were once as smooth and unmoving as stones, life emerges, begetting life.

It's as Hannah Whitall Smith says:

You have trusted the Lord Jesus for the forgiveness of your
sins and know something of what it is to belong to the
family of God and to be made an heir of God through
faith in Christ. Now you feel the longing to be conformed
to the image of your Lord. You know there must be an
entire surrender of yourself to Him, that He may work in
you all the good pleasure of His will. And you have tried
over and over to do it but up until now without any appar-
ent success. Come once more to Him, in a surrender of
your whole self to His will.[186]

And in the midst of the pecking and the sweating, in this
cramped place where we're all legs and arms and restless yearning,
this is where the surrender happens. Like Jacob, we wrestle doubt.
We work it out with fear and trembling, knowing we will get there.
If we keep on. We will reach the open space. If we don't give up.

This broad space is not a physical place free of masks or restric-
tions or lockdowns. No, in fact, it cannot be reached by human
feet. It's a place in the soul, trod only by prayer and worship, a place
reached by intercession and longing and hunger.

Hunger for real food.

Hunger for real drink.

Hunger for Jesus.

And when a congregant finally breaks free, he sings a song
with God, lifting up his voice so the rest of the hungry ones can
hear him: "Come, church, come, it's so glorious in this place of
trust! Come out and see!"

The pandemic is the incubator. It feels much like a lifeless
tomb, but the Lord uses it to form new hearts. It's only when we're
forced into the stillness, the darkness, that we get quiet enough to
need Him, and finally to hear Him.

People are dying from COVID-19. So many, every day. And even as my kids and I do homeschool, we pray together and make YouTube videos together, sharing the gospel. I order Bibles and send them to everyone I've ever known, because suddenly it's the only thing that matters.

This ancient scroll. And it strikes me one day, and I tremble: who is worthy to open it?

We fill bags with rolls of toilet paper and canned goods and candy, and we stick in gospels of John and handwritten cards. We go door-to-door giving love away; over our masks, our eyes shine like a lighthouse, pulling people to shore.

And then we go downtown, to the inner city, two hours away, and we bring blankets, and the kids bring some of their stuffies, and we give them out, along with food and more Bibles. We pray with people, and they look into our eyes, and sometimes they cry. Because it's been so long since anyone has seen them.

But no matter how many Bibles we give, it never seems enough. The globe is on fire, and all we have is a garden hose.

I eat and sleep the gospel. The shell has shattered, and I see my Maker. But more than that, I see the chicks that are struggling. "Do something!" I cry.

But God is patient. He lets the birds peck.

He keeps singing, and we keep giving.

One hug, one roll of toilet paper, one Bible at a time.

2020 – INDIA

And in the midst of our giving out Bibles and not traveling, God whispers, *India*.

He says it in the middle of another lockdown.

It's fall. The fields have had a crew cut. The playgrounds sit empty. The earth has forgotten how to play.

There's the crunch, crunch of broken leaves. I'm walking, a mile past my driveway on a gravel road. The sky is as blue as an iris, like I'm inside the eye of God.

Then I hear Him.

I've prepared a pastor for you in India.

India is not Africa. India is Asia. This ministry is global?

I glance around as if God is hiding behind a tree or a tractor. I see nothing but gravel and sky.

Back home, I text the board. They say they'll pray.

Winter passes, a white smudge of cold and skiing and building snowmen.

Then spring, with a splash of puddle and my bright red rain boots.

And that's when the ministry website breaks down.

It breaks down hard. We scour the globe for someone smart enough to fix it and kind enough to do it for free.

My friend finds someone in Nigeria who ends up working on the site and fixing it beautifully. But in the meantime, my friend also finds someone in India who seems like he might be a promising contact. And even though we don't need the website fixed anymore, we ask this Indian man if he would perhaps meet with us over Zoom. In a country of over eight hundred million Hindus, there's about a 2 percent chance he might be a Christian.

Not only is this man a Christian, but he's the son of a pastor who is the son of a pastor.

He says he will pray about someone who might be able to help us start a ministry in India. A little while later, he recommends a guy named James. He's never actually met James. But somehow he's heard of him, says he's working in one of the holy cities up north.

It turns out James is from Africa. And he's working in India.

There it is—the transplant. The little green shoot of the shea tree.

James says yes, he'll Zoom with us. My vice president and I are on the call with him and his American fiancée, and we don't want it to end. They are the kind of people who immediately feel like family. We laugh hard, and James thanks us for loving Africa.

We pray, but we are sure. This is our guy.

This African in India.

2021 – USA

Lectio divina is the process of eating the Word. Of God feeding His children like a mother bird, beak to beak, the Truth chewed up and made palatable for us.

John of the Cross defined the four stages of lectio divina in this way: "Seek in reading and you will find in meditation; knock in prayer and it will be opened to you in contemplation."[187]

The moment we can travel again, we practice lectio divina as a board. We gather in a room in Texas with our Bibles open, mask-free, gasping for air and for Jesus. And our board secretary leads us, verse by verse, in her soft, melodic voice, taking morsels from Scripture; we pause, meditate on the picture she's painted, the scene, the sounds and smells of it, the ambience of the passage. We ponder the tone behind the words, the culture. Then we pray, and we read the Scripture again, and our secretary invites us to contemplate the meaning of the words, their personal application to us.

It reminds me of swirling wine in a glass, sniffing it, giving it space to breathe. The more you smell, the more you taste.

And we pray along with poet and hymn writer Mary Lathbury:

Break now the bread of life, dear Lord, to me,
as once you broke the loaves beside the sea.
Beyond the sacred page I seek you, Lord;
my spirit waits for you, O living Word.[188]

Lectio divina gives the living Word a chance to speak.

We continue to enter into the text, carefully, so as not to smudge the ink or meaning. We travel past the sentences into the ambiance of the biblical text.

Lectio divina doesn't rush through a meal, like my army-trained husband does. It is a forced slowing. A resting in Logos. It's an enjoying, but also a respecting of the food laid before us. Of the One who prepared it.

Third-century theologian Origen of Alexandria believed the Word was incarnate in Scripture. Jesus living in the words, reaching out with pierced hands from Times New Roman font. This living and active two-edged sword, dividing joint and marrow, pit and fleshy fruit. This Lamb, taking the scroll between His hooves, His blood spilled so He can open the seals.

And even as we read and pause and chew and swallow, the Word tucks Himself into our hearts, makes a home in us, a place for birds to nest. We become one with Him as we ponder the truths throughout the day. They are nailed to the doorframes of our hearts, like a mezuzah, like the Word was nailed to the beams of the cross.

The Word made flesh through His words.

Moses says to plant Scripture—God's statues and commandments—inside our children. One translation puts it:

"You shall whet and sharpen them so as to make them penetrate, and teach and impress them diligently upon the [minds and] hearts of your children, and shall talk of them when you sit in your house and when you walk by the way, and when you lie down and when you rise up."[189]

So, basically, we are to talk about God's law and love all the time.

I used to feel it was forced, this eating and drinking God. It used to be homework. Lying there as a little girl under my thin sheet and my faded comforter, the streetlights blinking outside my window, my sisters asleep in their beds. I would leave prayer to the very last, the long rote of names, like the tassels on the Jewish leaders' robes, dangling. I prayed for each name, that they wouldn't die and go to hell; then I prayed for myself, that I wouldn't die and go to hell. But I forgot to pray that we would know how to live.

Stepping into each verse through lectio divina is like meeting Jesus on the mountain with Peter and James. I camp out on the grass, smell the sweat on Jesus's skin, watch it glow with glory. And I pray, "Teach me how to live, Lord."

I still pray for the ones going to hell, too; in fact, I can't stop praying for them. It's like a hurting in my chest, all squished up and aching, longing to stretch its limbs and run around and be free. It's like a chick in an egg.

I imagine this is what heaven will be like: love, running around, finally free.

"Leaping…from the stall."[190]

2021 – CANADA

The drop-in center reminds me of heaven. It's home for those who sing off-key and play harmonica and knit throw rugs and try to get off drugs. I come here weekly to lead Bible study.

Carl brings his dog in on a leash, a big dog that barks in your face then licks your hand. Carl looks strung out. He always smiles a slow smile. He shows me all his tattoos, even the ones I don't want to see. Carl is the one with the shattered heels from jumping off a balcony two stories up. Shrooms make you think you can fly. Carl's trying to fly away from a car accident that stole his best friend.

When I give him a Bible he sticks it in his boot, says he'll read it later. Then he stops coming to the center for a while, and I get worried. When he finally shows up again, he joins my Bible study but says the guy's voice on the video is weird. It freaks him out. After that he stops coming for a long time. When he finally returns, he looks more strung out than ever and doesn't want to talk anymore.

The center hides in a store called Flower Main. I always thought it was a flower shop until one day God told me to go in. So I went in and introduced myself. The flowers turned out to be people. They slapped me on the back and told me I'd dropped something. "Your shadow!" they said with a laugh. They were noisy flowers who swore and cried and said the same thing over and over until someone assured them they'd been heard. Some call it mental illness. I call it humanity.

At the drop-in, we always eat together. There's a big rectangular table. Every lunchtime people come and grab heaping plates of macaroni and cheese or lasagna, and they sit together and shovel food into their mouths like they're starving. For some, they are. This will be their only meal of the day. For others, like my friend Tyler, it might be his fifth.

The meal costs five bucks, but if they don't have the money they can still eat.

One lady colors in a coloring book while she eats. Brandon constantly talks about his piano, how it's too big. My friend Geoff tells people they need to buy a leprechaun and asks, "Wouldn't you like to be an alien?" When my daughter comes to visit, he asks her if I water her because she's growing like a plant.

Then there's Dan, who never remembers my name but holds my hand and says, "Halloween?" or whatever the upcoming holiday is, because he loves holidays. And he loves Jesus, too, so when I play guitar for Bible study, he sings loud. He shouts "Amen" at the end of the prayer, gives me a high five, and sometimes starts his own prayer for his mom and his cat and his favorite city.

People gather on couches when I read *The Jesus Storybook Bible*. Some of them get up and leave in the middle of the story, but most of them listen real quiet. Sometimes at the end they'll say, "Wow, God did that?" or, "That's so sad, hey? That's so sad"—like Brenda did at the end of the crucifixion story.

Here, Truth is chewed up and made palatable.

Luke is a single dad, a recovering addict who has a baby he sometimes brings to the center. One day, his baby laughs. We all stop what we are doing when it happens.

"A baby's laughing!" someone says. It sounds like a miracle.

My friends and I start doing evening church there once a month, and we bring potluck and Geoff brings his harmonica.

But even as we try to do church, it feels like things are a bit backward. Because church is already happening at the drop-in center. And we're just there to notice it. Love is already happening; it's not neatly listed in a bulletin as part of the order of service. It's unfiltered and messy. It's singing loud, even as we peck at our shells.

Church has a table at its center. A big rectangular one.

And salvation is wrestled out in this place where people are so openly sinners and so ready to be forgiven. They teach me how to repent.

Conner says over and over how much he's messed up his life. He knows about Jesus but doesn't quite get how salvation works. When I ask him if he wants Jesus to forgive his sins, however, he yells, "Yes, oh yes, please," and he starts the sinner's prayer with me and finishes it by stuffing chips in his mouth.

And even as I drop him off at his house, he starts beating his head, saying, "I shouldn't have gone out today, I shouldn't have." I tell him not to listen to the bad voices. I remind him he is forgiven. And he nods his head, and I tell him we love him, and he says, "I love you, too," and then he walks alone into his house.

Tyler is over six feet tall and weighs maybe three hundred pounds. His T-shirts are often too small and his glasses are broken. We tape them up. Tyler is a recovering addict. During supper he gives me his pipe and his weed and asks me to dispose of them. Then, during the church service, Tyler pulls me aside. We go sit on the couches behind the billiards table.

"How do I worship a God I can't see?" Tyler asks. "I want to worship Him, but it's hard."

"I know," I say.

He pushes up his glasses.

"I did see God though, once," he says. "I saw Him at Bible camp when I was young. I entered that camp and I heard someone laughing behind me. And then all of a sudden, I started laughing, and I didn't stop laughing the whole night. Like, I felt so much joy. It just filled me, you know?"

He stops. "I want that again, you know? I want to laugh again."

I pray for him, right then and there. I pray that he will laugh again.

Later I find out that he does. A few days after I pray for him, Tyler opens his Bible. He begins reading the book of John. As he reads, he starts to laugh. He laughs for three hours straight.

The Bible is powerful like that. It's a love letter. It sneaks up on you like a bear hug. And this love, it holds you, until you can't resist anymore, and you just have to laugh.

This love that sings over us. This love that holds the world.

fish

It is good enough to talk of God whilst we are sitting here
after a nice breakfast and looking forward to a nicer
luncheon, but how am I to talk of God to the millions who
have to go without two meals a day? To them God can only
appear as bread and butter.
—Mahatma Gandhi[191]

2021 – SRI LANKA

And then there are the ones too hungry to laugh.

Like the mothers of Sri Lanka.

They live on a tiny island known as the teardrop of India. They can't afford food for their children. Many of their babies are born with abnormalities because even the mothers' placentas are starving.

It didn't used to be this way. Sri Lanka was an up-and-coming country wowing the world with its economic prowess. Little did everyone know, it was feasting on empty dishes. The World Bank warned the government of Sri Lanka its investments were unsustainable and inequitable. Then, COVID-19 happened.

It's easy to collapse a country propped up by toothpicks.

I learn of Sri Lanka from my friend Maggie, a woman who wrote a theological curriculum that we quickly adopted for our work with local pastors. We'd been praying for a workable Bible curriculum for years.

In many places around the world, it's hard to equip communities through the local church because the church itself is unequipped. Countless pastors don't even own Bibles. Some possess just scraps of Scripture. Many haven't finished high school. Almost none of them have any kind of theological training.

In 2018 over six thousand churches in Rwanda were shut down by the government because the pastors didn't have a theology degree. Yet the few Bible colleges that exist in Africa cost more than a village pastor could ever afford.

These Bible courses, however, are free. And the thin piece of paper awarded at the end, that simple American diploma, is strong enough to keep a church from folding.

Maggie tells us that thousands of students in Sri Lanka have graduated from the program.

But now the country is starving to death. God's whisper to us is clear.

We are learning this: the world is very small to God. It's much like a baby to Him, and you can't love the toes of a baby without loving its head, without loving its fingers. You love all of a baby. And so we love all of the world. Country by country, toe by toe.

We fast now for Sri Lanka, for forty days. We make room in our hearts for this new place, for these mothers who once ate curry and jackfruit and salted fish, but who now eat maybe one bowl of rice a day. The cost of food has inflated by 80 percent. There's no paper for kids to take school exams. Fuel lines stretch for miles, and people have stopped going to church because they can't afford the gas.

I weep as I wept the first time I went to Uganda those many years ago.

I keep seeing her. The mother of my sponsor child. The one who, back in 2014, walked for four hours just to meet me. She'd worn a smile that was careful, like she was hiding her teeth. Her eyes were lowered. Eventually, though, she looked at me. And she laughed. Her mouth fully open, her soul fluttering out like a yellow butterfly.

Her fingers were calloused. She was a peasant farmer, she said. She worked sunup to sundown yet couldn't afford to send her kids to school. Women in Uganda aren't paid as much as men, and her husband had just died of AIDS. So when a children's home run by Westerners offered to take her children, she had felt she had no choice.

We sponsored one of her sons, John Mark. I'd brought him scribbled pictures from my kids. A family photo. A children's Bible. And John Mark had looked at me with eyes that shone.

But I wanted him to look at his mother that way. Not me.

And I want the children of Sri Lanka to look at their mothers that way too.

These women with their calloused fingers.

It's been months of praying for an opening for us to work in Sri Lanka.

I have no more leads. I've reached out to multiple contacts in both India and Sri Lanka. No one follows through. All dead ends.

I begin to worry I've misled my team. We've declared in faith we're going to help the mothers of Sri Lanka. Have we heard wrong?

Then, in a vision late at night, I see it.

A candle. And then, an Asian woman holding the candle. She gently takes my hand, guides me down a narrow, bumpy path in the dark. As we walk, other Asian women holding candles join us. They hum softly, a beautiful song. Then we come to a clearing, still in the dark, and there is a throng of women, a sea of candles.

The women are all singing.

After the vision, I wait for God.

A starving person forgets what hunger feels like.

The stomach stops crying, like an orphaned baby who knows no one is coming.

I remember when I was in the hospital and first started to feed myself again. My stomach was the size of a shriveled grape. It took time to stretch it out, like old pastry.

But you can't stretch out your stomach if you don't have any food.

Her name is Prisha. Her husband is a friend of James. They live in India.

I'd reached out to James's friend in desperation to see if he knew of someone from Sri Lanka. He'd immediately responded, "Oh! Yes. My wife is from Sri Lanka. She'd love to talk to you."

We're talking, now, over Zoom. Her smile is constant. Her little girl keeps poking her head into the camera frame to see me.

Prisha's childhood village is suffering. She has been praying for six months for God to send help for her people.

I have been praying for six months for God to lead us to someone in Sri Lanka.

So we pray together, and we ask God for a plan. Slowly, it forms. We've never done this kind of thing before, this emergency ministry. Normally we do long-term sustainable projects, not hand-to-mouth provision.

But we're staring into the eyes of an emaciated country.

Food is the only solution.

So we feed.

Prisha, along with her pastor and his wife, develop a grocery list for twenty village mothers and their children. Rice, flour, sugar, dahl, tea powder, chili powder, turmeric, biscuits, tin fish, garlic, jam, milk powder, and more. We begin to provide these items monthly for all twenty families. We commit to making these provisions for one year.

In the meantime, the mothers study the Bible together.

They put babies on laps, balance papers and pens, and study and take exams together.

This feeding of body and soul.

Once they've regained some strength, we go further.

Prisha meets with the mothers, discusses sustainable projects. Each mother shares her secret dream for a small business: tailoring, goat rearing, hairdressing, chili-powder processing. Budgets are set, God provides the funds, and Prisha helps each woman set up her own project.

After all, by the end of the year, each mother will need to be able to provide for her own family.

Her children looking up at her with shining eyes.

Sometimes you have to squint to see the wind.

Stewart Edward White says, "I have always maintained that if you looked closely enough you could *see* the wind—the dim, hardly-made-out, fine débris fleeing high in the air."[192]

But is that all wind is? Just fine debris?

Isn't it more like the breath of God?

Isn't it more of a pregnancy-inducing power, blowing where it pleases, picking up and dropping off disciples, moving mountains into seas?

And what if hearing is also a kind of seeing?

What if all these "whispers" in the dark from Jesus are actually keyholes into His majesty? What if the Word is in fact Sight? No one has seen God, but He tucked Elijah into the crevice of a rock and then whispered to him. And that whisper roared above the storm and fire, and it shattered the doubt that made Elijah want to die.[193]

I read an article that said, "The brain can, if it must, directly use sound to see and light to hear."[194]

Sound to see. Like Tyler "seeing" God at camp, when in fact he had heard God's laughter.

Where eyesight is poor, scientists say, the ears "pick up the slack" and act as eyes, stimulating the visual system. It's a form of synesthesia.[195]

A friend once told me she could see angels. I was sixteen and a Bible Director at a children's summer camp. She was a counselor. Whenever we walked into the chapel, she saw them. Angels in the rafters. I squinted and squinted but couldn't even catch the flash of a wing.

Most of us hear God rather than see Him. Not usually audibly. Often, through the Word—the Bible, its promises and parables. But one way or another, His voice is made known.

"My sheep hear My voice."[196]

And then, there is the even rarer form of synesthesia. The kind where people can taste words.

Only five people in the past century have been documented to have this "word-gustatory synesthesia."[197] One man who has it says Christmas "tastes like crisps dipped in plain yogurt."[198]

This makes me wonder: When they say His name, what does Jesus taste like to people with word-gustatory synesthesia? This One who is the Word? Does He taste like bread and wine? Or perhaps macaroni and cheese?

At the end of the year I visit the mothers in Sri Lanka. All of them are prospering, all of them have graduated from Bible school, all of them are feeding their children.

We take Communion together, the bread flaky and white, soaked red in the juice.

And one of them says to me, hands folded, eyes shining, "Jesus tastes so sweet to me. I keep opening my mouth wide, wanting to taste Him more. He's like the leaves of a tree that grows here. Its leaves are so sweet. Jesus tastes like that, and I can't stop eating Him."

Moses climbed the mountain saw God's glory. The rest of us beg God to take His glory from us—because it burns.

But Moses spent days in a tent before climbing the mountain. Before he saw, he trained himself to hear. Scripture says that when he emerged from the tent, his face glowed. Because for him, hearing was seeing.

Are we in training? Are we in our sukkot in the wilderness, beneath the palm and brush? Are we willing to look like lunatics to the outside world, willing to fast from our other senses, willing to let our eyes become bigger than our stomachs so we might hunger for something only light can fill?

During Lent and Advent my family and I fast from things like coffee and video games and chocolate and television. During these times we play board games together, we memorize Scripture together, we worship together, and we get along better.

When you empty yourself of the mundane filling-up, and your only go-to becomes falling at the feet of the Father, your other senses start to heighten. You begin to see what you used to only hear. You start to crave what isn't physical. You begin to listen with the ears of your spirit, to see with the eyes of your spirit. You begin to hear and to see and to taste God, who is Spirit.

During one of these family fasts, we read the story of William Seymour, the man who started the Azusa Street Revival. He was blind in one eye, this son of a slave. Because of his skin color, he wasn't allowed to attend Bible school alongside the other students. So, instead, he sat outside the classroom taking notes. And God began to use him. He used him in Los Angeles in 1906 to spark a revival that spread the Pentecostal movement worldwide.

The reason for William Seymour's success was his humility. For three years, upward of fifteen hundred people packed nightly into the small mission, and during those prayer meetings, William would be seated at the front—his face inside a wooden box.

"When William put his head in the box there was a glow that appeared around it. It was just like Moses' face used to shine after he had spoken with God and like Jesus' face shone in the transfiguration."

Whenever William pulled his head from the box the meeting would pause, for the people would know God had given him a message.

During those meetings, over three thousand tumors were healed, missing legs grew back, the lame walked—and, at one point, thirty-five deaf people were simultaneously healed, even as they held hands and prayed together.[199]

Yet for all the miracles, William remained blind in one eye. Perhaps because God knows blindness can be a gift.

Seymour could see things no one else could. He could see angels.

I'm sitting in an airport in Sri Lanka, waiting for my flight, feeling very grateful and pondering this verse from Acts: *"We were those who ate and drank with him after he rose from the dead."*[200]

That's how I feel when I go on these trips. Like I've eaten and drunk with our risen Lord Jesus. I feel full.

2022 – LIBERIA

I'm in a church in Barziwen Town, Liberia. Wrapped in a traditional robe, I'm seated in a plastic chair at the front of the room. On one side of me is Ibrahim and on the other, James. It's hot with the heat of a hundred bodies crammed together.

We're at a Bible school graduation.

The crowd is dotted with heads wrapped in African scarves, a fabric bouquet. The air smells like perfume and sweat. A million sounds compete: the scurrying of lizards underfoot, the caw-cawing of birds in the trees, the crowing of roosters that somehow think it's still dawn, the screeching of monkeys.

There's a lot of waiting here in Africa, but in the waiting is the witnessing of life. Insects that zip and zither. The sun's slow slide beneath the horizon. Children who tug on my skin like it's freckled cloth.

Finally the graduates file in wearing their black gowns and caps. They duck their heads, shy, the crowd cheering and throwing money at them. They find their places at the front.

There are introductions, a song. And then the valedictorian stands and speaks. He's slender with a black goatee and wears gold wire-rimmed glasses propped on his forehead. He tells us he prayed for a school like this for ten years. On days when classes were held, he walked five hours to the school, rising at three in the morning so he could arrive by eight, then turned and walked five hours home before dark. Most other days, he rose at two in the morning to study before working in the fields. And he earned a grade point average of 89 percent on all twenty-one courses. We clap till my palms nearly bleed.

Later I give a Certificate of Valor to a woman who walked three and a half hours each way to class, even after her husband died mid-course.

And I think of the words of other Liberian students, the ones from Bomi County, men and women who'd waited for hours for us to arrive. When we finally did they fairly exploded from their chairs and said, "Mama Emily, there's fire in our feet. We want to take back West Africa for Jesus."

I look at my feet now. They're pink and swollen. They're burning up.

"How beautiful on the mountains are the feet of those who bring good news...."[201]

Oh, that we would step closer to the mountain. Oh, that we would feel the burn. And oh, that the fire would make us run.

To the very ends of the earth.

oil

We cannot separate our lives from the Eucharist;
the moment we do, something breaks.
—Mother Teresa[202]

2022 – SIERRA LEONE

I'm learning a new kind of Christianity. One that smells like sweat and laughs a bit too loud.

The Bible is multidimensional to me now. I stumble over its translucent pages with the fishermen of Galilee.

Faith, I'm learning, is "not a pathetic sentiment, but robust vigorous confidence built on the fact that God is holy love," as Oswald Chambers says.[203]

God's holy love holds me, like the earth holds a seed.

It holds me as I climb into a hand-hewn canoe to cross Little Scarcies River in Sierra Leone. Crocodiles roam these rivers. On the other side, I follow Ibrahim up the mud path. The leaves are wet. We pass through a jungle they say is cursed, and we arrive at a tiny village where the huts have thatched roofs. One of the villagers holds a pet monkey on a rope. We sit on a broken bench and people gather. One brings a chicken.

Ibrahim greets everyone, exchanges pleasantries, asks if I have a word for them.

God gives me this:

> But now, this is what the LORD says—
> he who created you, Jacob,
>   he who formed you, Israel:
> "Do not fear, for I have redeemed you;
>   I have summoned you by name; you are mine.
> When you pass through the waters,
>   I will be with you;
> and when you pass through the rivers,
>   they will not sweep over you. [204]

Ibrahim looks at me and says, "That's perfect, ma'am. They're terrified of the river. They say demons live in it. That's perfect."

I hadn't known they were scared of the river. But God knew.

They give us the chicken and wide toothy smiles.

We continue through the jungle, down paths winding around fields. Boys stand in maize fields, shooing away birds, keeping them from eating the harvest. They wave at us with thin arms, shirtless and shoeless and happy. I'm sure they'll be the first to see Jesus when He returns. After all, they're always watching the sky.

We walk through tunnels of vine and tree. Finally we reach a very poor village, one of the many forgotten places this side of the river. Ibrahim is the only one who comes here bringing support and supplies: medicine, spray for bedbugs, cement for building churches, motorbikes for pastors he's placed here—all of it carried by canoe.

We preach to the ones who've gathered. But I know, somehow, the one really listening is the blind man we passed, the man still leaning against his hut. He didn't come to the meeting, but he can hear us, and it's to him I speak. He's not a believer—none of these people are. But I talk of the God who sees them, right here, the One who's not forgotten them. In this place with no electricity, I speak of the Light of the World.

Later, when I go back to Canada, Ibrahim will return to this village, and the blind man will be the first to accept Jesus. The first to see. The rest of the village will soon follow.

On our way back to Little Scarcies River, through the tunnels of vine and tree, we meet a farmer and his son. The man begins exclaiming and shouting. At first I think he's mad, but then I realize he's just excited. He says we're the ones who'd told him about his past. We're the ones who'd told him things he had told no one. And we're the ones who'd brought the nurse who bandaged his son's leg. Now his son's leg was healed.

It had happened the year before, in Ibrahim's village. I'd brought a friend who was a nurse, and I'd also brought our board secretary. We'd announced a health clinic, and before daybreak, the villagers and people who'd traveled there from other areas had lined up in front of Ibrahim's farmhouse; some had walked for hours from the forgotten places.

The clinic was just a simple set-up on Ibrahim's front porch, a table spread with antiseptics and bandages and over-the-counter pain relievers. The secretary and I pulled up chairs to pray over those in line.

All day, as the nurse bandaged wounds and administered medicine, we prayed over the people. Miraculously, God showed me things about their pasts. It was as if they were fruit left too long in the sun, and God was peeling them open, showing me their soft insides, their stories. He showed me things only He could have seen, and when I told them, they cried. They'd met *El Roi*, "the God who sees me."

This man remembers. And he can't stop thanking me.

Even as we stand there, we notice his son's sandals are broken. There's nowhere to get new ones, and they have no money. So Ibrahim and I fight over which one of us will give away our shoes. "Let me be the one to be blessed!" Ibrahim says, joking. But across the river, I've got a suitcase full of flip-flops. So I get to give. And somehow my shoes fit the boy's feet.

And he is radiant.

The ground feels soft to my bare soles.

I get to do this. I get to witness God's love for the forgotten.

And more than that, I get to be loved by them.

This girl—who once felt unseen, forgotten; all broken and empty, who ached to belong—now has a family so big there aren't arms long enough to embrace them all.

My first visit to Liberia, I walked with Pastor Victor across a broken bridge. We were met by members of his church, all smiles and singing and dancing, and they led us to their building and they hugged me. They clothed me in a fine gown, then told me in pidgin English, "Listen, Mama Emily. This be your home now. We be your family now. You never be alone again."

2023 – CANADA

I'm seated in my living room, piles of books—"world after world after world"[205]—on either side of me. A dozen worlds topple nearby, and one world rests, earmarked, in my hand.

It's late, and I shut my eyes for a moment—or "visit the backs of my eyelids," as Ibrahim would say.

In that moment, I see it: Christianity as it has become—a flat, tract-like thing. I see that it's dying, this form of our faith, this two-dimensional, shapeless thing, folding in on itself. And then I see that it won't truly die, that it cannot, for, like origami, I watch it transform into a fig.

And I understand why.

It's legend, they say, but perhaps the fig tree that broke through the tomb begs to differ.

There are different versions of the story, but one of the most common is that an atheist, a naval officer named Ben Wangford, who lived in Victorian times, was buried with a fig seed in his tomb.[206] Wangford wanted to know—even in death—whether or not God was real. He determined that if the fig could germinate, grow, and burst through the burial place, then it would show that God existed.

And so, upon Wangford's death, a fig seed was apparently tucked into his tomb. It indeed germinated, then grew into a tree that broke through the lid of the grave. The fig tree became a tourist attraction until the tree finally died in the 1960s.

Whether this story is legend or not, God is very much alive.

The thing about the fig is this: it isn't actually a single fruit. It's a holder, a pod, for hundreds of edible flowers. And each flower, in turn, holds a seed. So when you eat one fig, you're actually eating many figs, all at the same time.

It's like us, and all the seeds we hold: the promises in the Word, many future generations of saints. We are pods. We appear one, but, in fact, each of us is many.

I fold up my blanket, put away the books, lock the doors; I pray over the children, asleep in their beds, and I see it: this new kind of Christian, this seed, once buried, once cursed, along with the fruitless fig tree.[207]

It feeds on what remains, on the dry bones. It feeds on a secret, hidden power, the kind that lives underground. And that seed becomes a tree, which ultimately shatters the rock.

This new kind of Christian is so full of life and power, the grave cannot contain him.

Much like Christ, who was nailed to a tree so He could feed the whole world.

I crawl beneath the covers now, my own farmer by my side. Already Trent is picking out garden seeds. Soon he will plant them indoors, place them by windows, water them each day. When the roots are a tangled mass of white threads, he will transfer them to bigger pots, and finally, when the earth is warm enough, he'll move them to the garden. And there we will visit "our children," as we call them, walking among the rows, hand in hand, marveling over new buds and flowers and eventually the food offered up by the hands of these once-seeds. Seeds that died so we might live.

"He who works with the earth from whence he came and to which he will return gets healed of his wounds," writes Doherty. "He becomes deeply reconciled with God, and walks with Him at eventide while they both look over the creation of their hands."[208]

Lying there in bed, I pick up a book on revival by Dutch Sheets. I gasp as I read, "The greatest Farmer the world has ever known is pursuing the greatest harvest the world has ever seen!"[209]

The book goes on to say, "We are the generation of believers with the incredible privilege of reaping the greatest harvest of souls into the kingdom of God since the cross. Actually more than all other generations combined."[210]

And then I read, "Don't you just love it when the Lord takes dead religion, often paralyzed by powerless tradition or seemingly meaningless ritual, and infuses it with life?"[211]

Again, it's the flat, two-dimensional piece of religion, thrown into a tomb to die. It becomes Isaiah's Branch,[212] rising up. It splits through the stone of hearts and turns into a canopy, a refuge and hiding place from storm and rain.

Isaiah says humans themselves will become *"a shelter from the wind and a refuge from the storm."*[213] People, walking around like trees. Maybe the blind man had it right the first time.[214]

I want to shout hallelujah. I whisper it instead.

I feel the souls of the world grieving. I feel them like they're babies in my womb, crying. I see their faces like the one of the atheist, pleading, even as he's buried, to know the truth—to know if there is a God. And there is, and the fig proved this, but for him it was too late.

Just as it was for Mr. Ni's father.

Once a Buddhist leader, Mr. Ni was president of an idolatrous society and spent much time with the gods of China. But he was restless. When Hudson Taylor began sharing the gospel with him, about a God who loved the world so much He was lifted up like the snake in the desert, Ni said,

> I have long sought the Truth, but without finding it. I have traveled far and near, but have never searched it out. In Confucianism, Buddhism, Taoism, I have found no rest. But I do find rest in what we have heard tonight. Henceforth, I am a believer in Jesus.

He became an avid follower of Christ.

One day, Ni asked Taylor how long he'd had the gospel in his country back home. "Some hundreds of years," said Taylor.

"What! Hundreds of years?" Ni exclaimed. "My father sought the Truth and died without finding it. Oh, why did you not come sooner?"[215]

Even as we turn off the lights before going to sleep, Trent and I pray again for Turkey and Syria, where more than fifty thousand people have lost their lives in a massive earthquake and countless aftershocks. Buildings and bodies crumbling like the dust that they are; souls buried alive, some rescued after weeks—most, not. And all we can cry is, "God, reach them in the rubble. Reveal Yourself to them, even as You did to us."

Meanwhile, there's a stirring amid the shaking: a revival happening at Asbury College in Kentucky, much like the one that occurred in 1970. It started so simple, so small: with just twenty students, lingering after chapel service, and the worship leader telling them to pray over each other, to "become the love of God by experiencing the love of God," closing by asking God to "revive us by your love."

And love filled the room like oil in a jar. Students stayed long under the heavy palm of God, and when minutes turned to hours, others who'd gone to class came back, and then teachers and faculty came. And when hours turned to days turned to weeks, the world came. Pilgrims from north and south and east and west, to witness God, poured out in healings, in testimonies, in prayer, in worship.

For over two weeks hungry souls filled each of the fifteen hundred seats in the sanctuary, and those who couldn't sit, stood, lining walls and doorways, desperate to taste Him. Even as the death toll rose in Turkey and Syria, God's glory flowed in Kentucky like the waters from the temple, pouring out to the nations.[216]

Haggai prophesied on a feast day—on the day of the Feast of Tabernacles. This feast was to celebrate the wine and the oil harvest, the final great harvest of the year. But Haggai prophesied of a greater glory coming.[217]

Similarly, the prophet Joel said, *"The vats will overflow with the new wine and oil."*[218]

And Amos declared that the plowman would one day overtake the reaper, and the treader of grapes him who sowed the seed.[219] Meaning, the harvest will be so great it will be simultaneous with the planting—the hunger so much that even as people are being fed, the planting will need to take place to keep up, and the seasons will blur. Much like the dust behind a combine. The sower and the reaper glad, together.

2019 – LIBERIA

I'm a seed too, sewn in the secret place of love. My roots never leave the soil, yet Love takes me to the most fearful of places and holds me there.

I recall how it held me in Liberia, where a policeman at a checkpoint picked a fight with my taxi driver. I was on my way to the airport, at increasing risk to miss my flight the longer we were forced to wait.

No matter what our driver did—offering his license, his papers, a wad of money—nothing helped. The policeman became more irate.

All I could do was pray, "Lord, please send a man of peace."

Minutes later, a car pulled up beside us. A well-dressed African man stepped out. He approached my window, said, "Excuse me, ma'am, are you with the Peace Corps?"

I replied, "No, sir, I'm a missionary."

He nodded, stepped around the car, and addressed the policeman. "Excuse me, sir, is this how we treat our foreign guests?"

The policeman swallowed, lowered the rope. We were free.

I laughed.

"My cup runneth over."[220]

Holy laughter flowed, and it keeps flowing out of me as I travel the globe. I just laugh and laugh, like Tyler, at nothing really, but it is my spirit's mirth, the insides of me so full of joy they spill over.

benediction

*After eating the world's bread, we wake each morning to
remember: We are still hungry. Seek a better loaf. Eat, and
never die. Taste, savor, and be filled forever.*
—Calvin Miller[221]

2022 – EN ROUTE TO CANADA

My meal on the plane is long gone. The silver-haired man sleeps,
his glasses crooked, the pages of his book marked by a finger.

I finish *Babette's Feast*.

The sisters are discussing a party of sorts. They want to honor
the hundredth anniversary of their father's birth. It's an odd thing
to see two women garbed in black discussing a party. It's much like
a rain cloud discussing a sunrise, and yet here they are.

It's fall. The anniversary will be December 15. More than
a party, this celebration is a desperate plea to the lost souls of
their father's congregation, whose fellowship has been marred by

long-held offenses, grudges, and secret sins. The gathering will be an invitation to recall the dean's kindness of spirit. As the book describes, "It was as if the fine and lovable vigor of their father's personality had been evaporating, the way Hoffmann's anodyne will evaporate when left on the shelf in a bottle without a cork."[222]

The orphaned clan, toothless and hunched, are now petty and old. They dust off the pettiness and place it on the sisters' table like a vase of dead flowers.

In the meantime, a letter arrives for Babette. It's the first piece of mail she's received in twelve years. The sisters watch as she opens it, and Babette tells them that, each year, a friend in Paris has renewed her lottery ticket. This year, her number has won. She's now in possession of 10,000 francs!

As Martine and Philippa express their congratulations to Babette, they suddenly realize what this woman means to them—and that she will soon leave them.

One evening Babette approaches the sisters and reminds them she's never asked them for anything in all her years of service but would like to be granted one request—to prepare the meal for their father's birthday. Not just any meal: she wants to cook them a real French dinner. And not only that, but she wants to pay for it all herself.

The sisters are taken aback. They hadn't intended to serve anything but a light supper and a cup of coffee. But how can they refuse this woman who has faithfully served them for so long?

Over the next few weeks, boat after boat arrives with parcels of exotic food—including a huge tortoise. The sisters grow frightened of that which they don't know. They assume it's a witch's brew and repent to the members of their sect for allowing the dinner. The congregants are sympathetic; wanting to support the dear sisters, they agree that while they will still attend the dinner, they will not enjoy this meal or even talk about it.

The sisters learn that an unexpected guest will be present for the celebration—an old suitor of Martine's, now a general, who accompanies his aunt, a longtime supporter of the late dean's congregation.

The guests arrive and are seated. They are unified in their secret pact to not enjoy the food—all except the general, who progressively exclaims over every part of the exquisite meal.

Gradually the wine softens the hearts of the members of the small congregation. Those who have been feuding confess to each other and are reconciled.

Finally, overcome by the meal—for it resembles, exactly, a meal he had in Paris years ago where the chef, a woman, had been renowned as a culinary genius—the general rises. He speaks of grace—how shortsighted man's view of it is. But in truth, he says, grace has no limits. It demands nothing but that we wait for it boldly and accept it thankfully. Grace is abundance, he says, wanting nothing but to be needed and received.

A finer sermon had never been preached. It breaks wide the parishioners' hearts, and they stumble into the night, holding hands, falling like children into soft piles of snow.

The sisters find Babette sitting, exhausted, alone in the kitchen amid dishes and mess. They had forgotten to thank her, but they do so now. She then tells them she was once a chef at a famous restaurant in France. For she was, in fact, the culinary genius the general had spoken of.

The sisters seem not to hear her words, simply say they will remember the meal long after she's returned to Paris.

Then Babette tells them.

She won't be going back to Paris. She's spent all her money on the meal.

I weep, staring at the black rectangle of screen.

To me, Babette was Jesus.

She came to those who weren't her own. She came to those who thought they knew God. She came to serve them.

The sisters taught her, a culinary chef, how to make fish soup. Much like teaching God the alphabet.

"*Yet he did not open his mouth.*"[223]

They had prayed for her soul, while Babette had cooked for them and washed their dishes.

Her only request was to do more. To take all she had and spend it on one lavish meal she wouldn't even be a part of. A meal that would cost her everything.

2022 – SIERRA LEONE/LIBERIA

In Africa, I'm relearning food.

Ibrahim uses a knife, cuts the thick rind, digs in his teeth, then tears off the top of his orange like a lid. It's as if he's opening a jar of marmalade. He brings the mouth of the "jar" to his lips and sucks. The round fruit soon deflates, a popped balloon.

"That's how we eat oranges in Sierra Leone," he says. Wipes his chin with the towel on his shoulder.

I ask for a knife, and I peel. I make an opening with my teeth, try to suck dry the fruit, and it drips down my chin, all pulp and marrow.

It's delicious.

It's like I've never truly tasted an orange before.

Is this how Adam and Eve ate fruit in the garden? Not a care, just ripping tops off oranges and lemons, sucking them dry, casting the rinds aside for the animals, hand in sticky hand with God?

It's evening here in the village of Masaralie.

Mommy Mariama has fed us snap fish and couscous. Moths flap against the open screen. There's the faint smell of charcoal. The night sounds of a choir of cicadas and the quiet scuffle of animals, the hum of a generator.

Ibrahim's house is one of two in the village that have electricity, so people gather on his front porch, children bringing homework, and elders their stories. They huddle together like flies under the one dangling bulb. Light does that. It gathers.

A boy has a boil, and I bring bandages. The children watch as I wash his wound. They can't stop smiling.

"Ma'am, we've been embarrassed by your goodness," Ibrahim says to me. "Now it's our turn to bless you."

The next day we journey to Liberia. In Ibrahim's trunk, we carry a dead pig, wrapped up and ready for roasting. The plan is to stop at his house in Freetown to feast with the orphans. Instead, the car breaks down for good this time. So we climb on motorcycles, sending the pig by taxi to Ibrahim's house. We follow the road to the border; spend the night in Bo, in a guesthouse with hard beds.

We eat bread and fried egg for breakfast. Pastor Victor finds us there, and we squish together into a taxi. We drive pot-holed roads for hours, visit pastors, climb back in, drive some more. We sing hymns off-key and eat bananas. A boy jumps onto the roof of our car, and Ibrahim hands him a banana, and we continue, the boy riding on top.

"I love bananas," Ibrahim tells me.

"I know," I say. I'm distracted by the boy's dangling feet.

We follow a truck stuffed high with palm branches. On top of the branches sit a goat and two boys. I try not to stare.

At one point our taxi slows down and backs up. The driver starts yelling at a man. The man runs up, pulls a knife on our driver. I scream. They laugh, say they are joking. I tell them it isn't funny.

There's a semitruck packed high with produce, and a whole village of people on the top of the pile, their hands clinging to the ropes securing the fruit. The semi is pitching back and forth, reminding me of my grandmother's rocking chair, and I hear singing. The villagers are singing on top of the swaying semi.

This is Africa.

In Monrovia, Ibrahim calls a friend, a lady who cares for twenty orphans. She takes us in, feeds us heaping plates of food. We get to feast with orphans after all.

We wash, sleep, continue.

We cross checkpoint after checkpoint in our journey north. Some guards demand money; others let us through because Ibrahim says, in his deep voice, "Hello, sir, Reverend Ibrahim here. Retired police officer."

At one point the roads are so bad we see a semi stuck up to its roof in wet mud. So we climb onto motorbike taxis, ride them for eight hours.

We pass people carrying dried grass and piles of sticks and machetes and yellow jerry cans. I wave my white arm at the children, and they turn and wave back, like we're old friends.

Near the end of the trip we spend a night in a village. A family has given us their house. A woman with a kerchief is bleaching the plastered walls. Victor calls her Granny. She shows me my room: a mattress with a sheet on the floor, a candle in the corner. It's clean and warm and quiet.

I rinse off red dust using one of the pails of steaming water brought in by some church ladies. They've boiled it by hand over a charcoal fire. A bath is sacrifice here.

I pull on my sweats, step into the dining room. Candles drip from every corner. Ibrahim, Victor, and James are seated at the table by the door.

Suddenly the door opens and some elderly women enter. They shake a dried-gourd rattle, begin to sing and dance, old bones swaying. I feel like I'm eating the orange all over again, I'm so happy. I laugh and clap, and they sing and dance, white smiles floating like moths around the candlelit room. Then they hug me and leave.

We feast on rice and chicken and watermelon.

That night, on the mattress without a pillow, I dream. I dream of homes and families and churches and new life. I dream of the kingdom of heaven.

"Let there be light," God says, and stars fling from His mouth, stick against the black flannel of sky.

"Their starry host by the breath of his mouth."[224]

The darkness will never win. Corruption and bribery and betrayal will never win. It's all just a backdrop.

A black tablecloth, spread in the desert.

God's glory piled high like a feast for orphans.

Part Four:

Koinonia

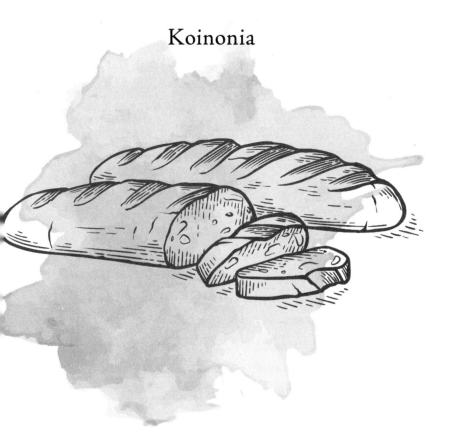

table

I want all of the holiness of the Eucharist to spill out beyond church walls, out of the hands of priests and into the regular streets and sidewalks, into the hands of regular, grubby people like you and me, onto our tables, in our kitchens and dining rooms and backyards.
—Shauna Niequist[225]

2023 – BURUNDI

He gapes at me with a gummy smile, this hundred-year-old pastor from Burundi. I grin back, and he chuckles. His eyes squint into slits as he leans forward. A song trickles out from tired lips. The smallest song, the slightest trickle, from this ancient man.

God's name in Kirundi is *Mana*.

Here in the poorest country in Africa, where people often steal pig food to eat, where five-year-olds beg on the streets, where only one in ten pastors is trained, God's name sounds like the word

table 221

for the heavenly bread He caused to fall from the sky to feed His people.

Burundi is shaped like a heart, is called the "heart of Africa." It's also James's home country, where he grew up before the civil war chased him and his family to Kenya in 1993.

He remembers the militia in Kenya. He was five, stranded on a riverbank behind his church. He'd lost track of his family in all the chaos. The militia was closing in when someone grabbed him from behind, carried him across the river, and placed him with his mother.

In 2011 his family returned to Burundi. I'm in his family's living room now with half a dozen regional pastors from across the country. We're gathered together, our first night here.

At first it is quiet and hot. It's the kind of hot that presses like an old steel iron. I am told to sit on a chair by the table. The rest sit on couches, and they don't talk, and the heat presses.

James's dad, Pierre, sleeps. His head droops onto his priest's collar, his gold cross hangs lopsided across his purple dress shirt.

Then James brings in two fans, and his mom, Deborah, calls us to the table. There is a stirring. Pierre wakes and prays, and Deborah lifts aluminum lids like curtains from pans: reveals peas, cheesy potatoes, pork, steamed *matoke*, groundnut sauce, and fish from Lake Tanganyika. And there is bread: a round steaming loaf made from cassava flour, still doughy—like *posho*—so hot, yet fingers still dig in and twist, pull. The bread is used to mop up sauce, to ladle food, to eat.

Dessert is fresh pawpaw, or papaya, long fleshy strips still attached to the rind, baby bananas, green oranges.

Pierre pushes back his chair. He praises God. "When you're full, that's when the tongues begin," he'll say later.

We retire to the living room, where Pierre pulls out the red wine and pours. In this land of severe fuel shortage, where cars line up for miles to get gas, many of these pastors have had to sell a pig to cover their transportation costs. But while they're here, they will feast.

The ancient pastor with the gummy smile stands, shaky, on thin legs. He's dressed in a burgundy faux-leather jacket and blue slacks, and he begins to sing and dance.

The other pastors leap to their feet, start rhythmic clapping, and their voices break into a torrent of choruses, an acapella harmony unlike any I've ever heard.

"Africa doesn't have much," Pierre says, "but it has singing."

He directs the group like a maestro, one glass of wine in his hand, the other keeping time, and he too begins to dance.

I don't understand the words, but my spirit knows it's worship. My hands lift. I close my eyes, and I toast my glass to the God who is Manna.

This, the most joyous communion.

Later, the songs subside. James and I share about The Lulu Tree; a pastor falls asleep, lulled by the wine and the fans. Then I hand out audio Bibles. The men marvel over the little machines, pushing a simple button to discover Scripture playing in their native tongues of Kirundi and French. For men who have only one Bible for their entire congregation to share, this audio player is gold.

And even as Scripture plays from half a dozen speakers, it reminds me of the story of a Huguenot family in France during the sixteenth century.

It was a time when the French Catholic government persecuted Protestants. It was a time when owning a Bible was illegal. Knowing soldiers were going to raid their home, the Fasquet

table 223

family hastily baked their Bible into a loaf of bread. The Word, hidden in—even made—food.

Then there's the story of the LeFevre family from northeastern France. In 1685, Sarah LeFevre wrapped their Geneva Bible in vellum, then baked it in a huge loaf. Soon afterward, soldiers raided their home and slaughtered every member of the family except for their sixteen-year-old son Isaac, who was away at the time. When he came home and saw what had happened, he grabbed the loaf containing the precious Bible and ran to a friend's house. That night he escaped to Bavaria, a Lutheran state. The loaf traveled with him.[226]

Scripture clinging to dough, even as the Word clings to us.

"I am the living bread that came down from heaven," Jesus says.[227]

Do we consume true manna? Or are we the ones who keep seeking honey wafers, the kind that dissolve in the sun?

Yesterday I was in Uganda. We'd spent a week there celebrating the graduation of 127 Bible school students. During that time, we visited women and their small businesses, where they sew dresses and make jewelry. And there, in the pearl of Africa, in the place The Lulu Tree was born, one of my friends bought me a beautiful African dress. When I put it on, I twirled. Like a little girl. Then I wore it to church, and while I listened to my friend Emmanuel preach on how Christ is made manifest in every part of Scripture, Jesus made Himself manifest to me.

I didn't see the contours of His face. I just saw His bigness, His brightness, His all-consuming-ness, and I was lost in my smallness. But it was a comforting feeling, like I was being engulfed by a giant hand, by Love Himself, and all that mattered to this little girl was Him. He was my everything. I was consumed.

And even though my dress had been purchased in Uganda, when I looked at the tag, it said "Made in Burundi."

The wine glasses are topped up now, and the songs resume. Deborah pulls out her worn Bible, turns to Romans 7; and when things are quiet again, she exhorts the pastors to ponder this passage:

> *What a wretched man I am! Who will rescue me from this body that is subject to death? Thanks be to God, who delivers me through Jesus Christ our Lord!*[228]

We tuck this Scripture inside us so that, should pain or suffering break us in two, the Word will be found within this fleshy dough. The pages a bit scorched and water damaged.

The evening draws to a close. Glasses have been emptied and spirits filled. I pray over the pastors, and they wave their goodbyes, step from the room into the night. I don't know when I'll see them again.

They go, fleeing the militia of poverty and lack.

But they have One who carries them across the waters. And I'm pretty sure He's singing.

2023 – CANADA

"We'd hear the swish, swish and know she was up," Trent's aunt says. "She was mixing real cocoa, like a spoonful of cocoa, with a spoonful of white sugar, and then real cream from the cow. Then she'd wait until everyone got up, and she'd pour in the hot water."

She's talking about Trent's grandma.

We're seated for coffee now, plates of homemade banana muffins on the table, children with smeared chocolate on their lips. Outside the world is bright with snow and ice.

table 225

Trent's mom remembers the cups his grandma used to serve the cocoa. "They were kind of beveled on the side, little plastic cups, not very big."

I think of Communion. Of the swish, swish sound of the wine that causes souls to rise from sleep. Of the love that stirs.

"We cannot love God unless we love each other, and to love we must know each other," writes Dorothy Day. "We know Him in the breaking of bread, and we know each other in the breaking of bread, and we are not alone any more. Heaven is a banquet and life is a banquet, too, even with a crust, where there is companionship."[229]

Trent's grandma is in a nursing home now, and she doesn't eat much anymore. Cuisine has lost its taste, meals their intimacy, because food is served from cans.

"You can just hear the tins opening," the wife of a cousin says. "Tins don't make food taste very nice. I wouldn't want to eat it either."

They pull out recipes and talk about homemade sauerkraut and biscuits with buttermilk.

They talk about what they do on Sundays. Some of them make soup because they never know who's coming over. "You can always add more water to soup," Trent's aunt says with a laugh.

I think of *Fiddler on the Roof*, of the call to the Sabbath, of the candles and the laying out of food and the gripping of hands and the singing of the blessing.

It's as if each day of the week is leading up to the grand finale, to the eternal Sabbath or Feast Day.

It's as if all of our lives are a preparation for the banquet in the sky.

Mum no doubt will be dancing, Uncle Joe playing his fiddle, and the Spirit and the bride saying, *"Come."*[230]

This messianic feast.

But it is Christ who will fill us, like a Person stepping into us, like the flame from a candle consuming us, filling every broken part with light.

And we will come as eager children to the table.

Our heads drenched in oil.

Our hearts so very full—

Of this God who became bread.

Mum's Bread Recipe

7 cups warm water
3 tablespoons yeast
1 cup honey or ½ cup white sugar

(Blend the above for 10 minutes in a bread mixer.)

5 cups whole-wheat flour
½ cup butter
2 tablespoons salt
2 tablespoons vinegar

(Add to the first set of ingredients. Blend together for 10 minutes.)

5-plus cups all-purpose flour

(Add to the other ingredients and blend for 10 minutes.)

Remove dough from mixer and knead on a floured countertop for 3 to 5 minutes.

Place dough in a greased bowl, cover with a clean dish towel, and let rise about 1 to 2 hours until almost overflowing from the bowl.

Divide dough into five loaves. Place into greased loaf pans. Cover loaf pans with a dish towel and let rise again, about 1 hour.

Bake for 30 minutes at 350 degrees Fahrenheit.

Remove from loaf pans.

Butter the tops. Allow to cool.

Eat warm with strawberry jam or as desired.

Acknowledgments

A book is nothing but a germ, a lifeless cell, unless breathed on by the Holy Spirit and labored over by the writer and cheered on by spiritual midwives and mid-husbands.

This section is for those who cheered.

To my agent, Chip MacGregor, of MacGregor and Luedeke Literary: for never giving up on me, even when I gave up on myself. Thank you.

To my publisher, Whitaker House—specifically, Christine, Amy, and Lois: what a gift you are to me. You've become family, so quickly. Bless you for believing in this message and its messenger.

To my dear Wen: what pure joy to do this journey with you, my warrior friend. You teach me to trust Jesus, over and over again.

To Jeanne: you bring beauty wherever you go. I knew that if you believed in this book, I could. And you did. So I do too.

To Erica: your cheers can always be counted on. I don't know what I'd do without you.

To Steve: you were the one who made me think about writing again, that day we were stranded in northern Uganda. And you gave me the courage to do so. Thank you, friend.

To Norah: your prayers carry me, even as they carried this book. Thank you for always being there.

To the rest of my Lulu Tree team around the globe: thank you for loving me. Thank you for your sacrifice. I know God better because of you.

To Rebekah: my fellow herald. I cannot thank you enough for your conviction of spirit and your integrity of heart. This book and I are changed because of you.

To Tabitha: you brought much-needed order to this story. Bless you.

To my dad, Ernest: for teaching me all I needed to know. I love you.

To my handsome hubby, Trenton: for making me the woman I am today. For loving me through all the ugly. For always making me laugh. Your love is Christ to me.

To my wonderful children, Aiden, Kasher, and Aria: I'm so proud of you. You are the best part of my story. Thank you for letting Mommy write, edit, and edit some more.

And to the Trinity, without whom I would be but a germ, a lifeless cell: from You and through You and for You are all things. To You be the glory forever! Amen.

Notes

Dedication

1. Merriam-Webster.com Dictionary, s.v. "companionable," accessed November 6, 2023, https://www.merriam-webster.com/dictionary/companionable.

Epigraph: "Table Blessing"

2. "Table Blessing," © Jan Richardson, from *In Wisdom's Path: Discovering the Sacred in Every Season* (Orlando, FL: Wanton Gospeller Press, 2012), 129. Used by permission. janrichardson.com.

Preface

3. *The Little Way: Reflections on the Joy of Smallness in God's Infinite Love* (New Kensington, PA: Whitaker House, 2023), 128.

PART ONE: THE HUNGER

table

4. Frederick Buechner, *Listening to Your Life: Daily Meditations with Frederick Buechner*, comp. George Conner (New York: HarperOne, 1992), 261.

5. See 1 Samuel 21:1–6; Matthew 12:1–8.

6. John 6:56.

7. Luke 22:19 (NKJV).

8. See John 21:17.

bread

9. Dr. Rowan Williams, "Enthronement Sermon," February 27, 2003, Dr. Rowan Williams, 104th Archbishop of Canterbury, http://rowanwilliams. archbishopofcanterbury.org/articles.php/1624/enthronement-sermon.html.

10. See 1 Timothy 6:16.

11. Isaiah 29:8.

wine

12. Henri Nouwen, *The Living Reminder*, in *The Spiritual Life: Eight Essential Titles by Henri Nouwen* (San Francisco: HarperOne, 2016), 239.

13. John 4:10.

14. See verses 27–39.

15. See Luke 24:13–35.

16. Deuteronomy 32:14.

17. See, for example, Matthew 11:19.

18. See 1 Samuel 21:1–6.

19. See 2 Samuel 6:1–7.

20. Mark 5:31; Luke 8:45.

21. Anonymous, "For Health and Strength," circa 1850, https://hymnary.org/text/for_health_and_strength_and_daily_food.

22. See John 12:1–3.

23. See Matthew 12:1–14.

mangoes

24. Saul Williams, AZQuotes.com, Wind and Fly LTD, 2024. https://www.azquotes.com/quote/1511091, accessed April 1, 2024.

25. See Luke 16:19–31.

26. Job 1:21.

27. 1 Corinthians 11:24 (NKJV).

28. See Numbers 20:2–13.

29. Psalm 23:5 (KJV).

fish

30. Elie Wiesel, *Night* (New York: Hill and Wang, 2006), 52.

31. See Matthew 4:4; Luke 4:4.

32. Genesis 1:26.

33. See John 1:14.

34. Mark 5:41.

35. See Mark 5:43.

oil

36. "From Thomas Jefferson to George Wythe, with Enclosure, 16 September 1787," *Founders Online*, National Archives, https://founders.archives.gov/documents/Jefferson/01-12-02-0128. [Original source: *The Papers of Thomas Jefferson*, vol. 12, *7 August 1787–31 March 1788*, ed. Julian P. Boyd. Princeton: Princeton University Press, 1955, pp. 127–130.]

37. See Daniel 6:10.

benediction

38. Stephen King, *The Dark Tower I: The Gunslinger* (New York: Scribner, 2016), 176.

39. Isak Dinesen, *Babette's Feast*, in *Anecdotes of Destiny and Ehrengard* (New York: Vintage Books, 1993), 21.

40. Dinesen, *Babette's Feast*, 43.

41. Dinesen, 44.

42. Dinesen, 22–23.

43. Verses 10, 13–14.

PART TWO: THE FEAST

table

44. John Piper, *A Hunger for God: Desiring God Through Fasting and Prayer* (Wheaton, IL: Crossway, 2013), 25–26.

45. William Hammond, "Awake, and Sing the Song," 1745, https://hymnary.org/text/awake_and_sing_the_song.

bread

46. Margaret Atwood, *Selected Poems II: 1976–1986* (Boston: Houghton Mifflin, 1987), 53

47. Ephesians 4:10 NKJV.

48. Ephesians 3:19 NKJV.

49. See Ezekiel 3:3.

50. Madeleine L'Engle, *A Wrinkle in Time: 50th Anniversary Commemorative Edition* (New York: Square Fish), 194.

51. George Bennard, "The Old Rugged Cross," 1912.

52. Ephesians 1:23.

53. Exodus 24:11.

54. See Mark 7:24–30.

55. Madeleine L'Engle, *Glimpses of Grace: Daily Thoughts and Reflections* (New York: HarperOne, 1996), 28 (January 31).

56. John 12:24 ESV.

57. Psalm 85:10 KJV.

58. Deuteronomy 30:19 MSG.

59. Deuteronomy 32:47.

60. Hosea 2:14–15 AMP.

61. Hosea 2:23.

62. See verses 21–23.

63. See Ephesians 1:4, 6–7.

wine

64. Fyodor Dostoevsky, Goodreads, https://www.goodreads.com/quotes/search?q=dostoevsky+on+beauty.

65. 1 Corinthians 15:31 NRSVUE.

66. Revelation 3:20 KJV.

67. 1 Corinthians 15:42–44.

68. Gerard Manley Hopkins, "God's Grandeur," in *Poems and Prose*, reprint edition (Penguin Classics, 1985), 27.

69. Genesis 1:26 NKJV.

70. Genesis 1:29.

71. See John 6:53.

72. Isaiah 55:2.

73. See Hosea 11:3–4.

74. Thomas O. Chisholm, "Great Is Thy Faithfulness," 1923.

75. See 1 Corinthians 11:21–22.

76. Fulton J. Sheen, Goodreads, https://www.goodreads.com/quotes/7272680-broken-things-are-precious-we-eat-broken-bread-because-we.

77. John 19:28.

78. See John 19:30.

79. Psalm 19:3–4.

80. 1 Corinthians 15:40.

81. Ezekiel 37:5–6.

mangoes

82. Francis Chan, "My New Communion Views: Francis Chan Explains the Eucharist," Remnant Radio, YouTube video, 13:35, May 26, 2022, https://www.youtube.com/watch?v=2bH4hpCB2VU.

83. John 3:3.

84. See Psalm 18:9–10.

85. See Ezekiel 1:1–25.

86. See 1 Kings 18:41–45.

87. Luke 23:34.

88. Leviticus 23:17.

89. See, for example, Matthew 13:31–32.

90. Isaiah 25:4.

91. Psalm 119:103.

92. Psalm 119:20.

93. Brother Yun, *The Heavenly Man* (Grand Rapids, MI: Kregel Publications, 2020), 26–30, 33.

94. Isaiah 55:1.

95. Luke 14:21, 23.

96. Thérése of Lisieux, *The Little Way*, 53.

fish

97. Augustine, *Confessions*, 74.

98. See, for example, John 6:1–14.

99. See Matthew 15:29–39.

100. Isaiah 6:3.

101. See Revelation 4:8–11.

102. Ezekiel 1:24.

103. Hebrews 1:3.

104. Ezekiel 3:23.

105. See Revelation 5:6–10.

106. C. S. Lewis, *The Last Battle* (New York: HarperCollins, 1994), 213.

107. See Luke 12:22–32.

108. Lewis, *The Last Battle*, 228.

109. Amy Carmichael, *Gold Cord: The Story of a Fellowship* (Fort Washington, PA: CLC Publications, 2002), 123.

110. Lewis, *The Last Battle*, 209, 217, 219, 227.

111. See Judges 7:1–22.

112. Exodus 14:14.

113. Verse 4.

114. Rolland Baker and Heidi Baker, *There Is Always Enough: God's Miraculous Provision Among the Poorest Children on Earth* (Kent, England: Sovereign World Ltd., 2003), 49–50.

115. See, for example, Matthew 21:6–10.

116. See Luke 15:8–10.

117. See, for example, Matthew 18:10–14.

118. See Luke 15:11–32.

119. See 1 Corinthians 13:1.

120. Oswald Chambers, *My Utmost for His Highest* (Uhrichsville, OH: Barbour Publishing Inc., 1963), February 21.

oil

121. Smith Wigglesworth, *Smith Wigglesworth on the Anointing* (New Kensington, PA: Whitaker House, 2000), 41–42.

122. Catherine Doherty, *Apostolic Farming* (Combermere, ON: Madonna House Publications, 2001), 61, 67.

123. Doherty, *Apostolic Farming*, 89.

124. Brennan Manning, *The Ragamuffin Gospel: Good News for the Bedraggled, Beat-Up, and Burnt Out* (Colorado Springs, CO: Multnomah, 2005), 61.

125. Luke 19:5–9.

126. See, for example, Matthew 11:19.

127. See, for example, Matthew 26:6–13.

128. Manning, *Ragamuffin Gospel*, 59–60.

129. Ecclesiastes 3:20 NKJV.

130. See Luke 22:44.

131. Like 22:42.

132. Ho Man Tang and Ho Lam Tang, "Anastasis: Recovery from the Brink of Cell Death," Royal Society Open Science, published online September 19, 2018, National Library of Medicine, https://www.ncbi.nlm.nih.gov/pmc/articles/PMC6170572/#:~:text=Anastasis.

133. Luke 22:42.

134. Zechariah 14:8.

135. See Ezekiel 47:1–12; Revelation 22:1–2.

136. See Zechariah 14:4–21; Revelation 19:11–21.

137. See Colossians 2:15.

138. Ecclesiastes 7:2.

139. Verse 2.

140. Warren W. Wiersbe, *Be Satisfied: Looking for the Answer to the Meaning of Life*, OT Commentary, Ecclesiastes, 2nd ed. (Colorado Springs, CO: David C. Cook, 2010), 100.

141. See John 9:1–7.

142. Mother Teresa, "Mother Teresa,/Quotes/Quotable Quote," Goodreads, https://www.goodreads.com/quotes/8263642-i-held-the-host-with-two-fingers-and-thought-how.

143. See Zechariah 14:16.

144. Lauren F. Winner, *Girl Meets God: On the Path to a Spiritual Life* (Chapel Hill, NC: Algonquin Book, 2016), 13.

145. Zechariah 14:20–21.

benediction
146. Michael Flynn, *Eifelheim* (New York: Tor Books, 2006), 292.

147. Dinesen, *Babette's Feast*, 25–31.

148. See 2 Samuel 6:12–19.

149. See James 2:19.

PART THREE: THE FEEDING
table
150. Max Lucado, *Traveling Light: Releasing the Burdens You Were Never Intended to Bear* (Nashville, TN: Thomas Nelson), 36–37.

151. See 1 Kings 17:7–16.

152. See Mark 5:21–24, 35–43.

153. See John 12:2.

154. See, for example, Matthew 26:20.

155. Revelation 3:20.

156. See Luke 10:39–42.

bread
157. C. H. Spurgeon, "The Candle," April 24, 1881, Spurgeon Gems, https://www.spurgeongems.org/sermon/chs1594.pdf.

158. John 21:15–19.

159. See Acts 1:1–9.

160. See Acts 2.

161. See, for example, Matthew 26:14–16, 47–49.

162. Doherty, *Apostolic Farming*, 48–49.

163. Leonard Ravenhill, Facebook, December 6, 2019, https://www.facebook.com/ LeonardRavenhill/posts/it-is-all-right-to-say-i-want-to-be-like-jesus-but-do-you-want-gethsemane-i-have/10156895247711593/.

164. "Use Fish Scraps as Garden Fertilizer," Gardening Channel, https://www. gardeningchannel.com/use-fish-scraps-as-garden-fertilizer/.

165. See John 11:1–44.

166. Verse 44.

167. Luke 24:6.

168. Francis Chan, *Crazy Love* (Colorado Springs, CO: David C. Cook, 2013), 118.

169. Emily Dickinson, "Hope Is the Thing with Feathers" (254), Poets.org, Academy of American Poets, https://poets.org/poem/hope-thing-feathers-254.

170. Oswald Chambers, "The Discipline of Heeding," *My Utmost for His Highest*, February 14, https://utmost.org/classic/the-discipline-of-heeding-classic/.

171. Proverbs 26:2 NKJV.

172. Brother Lawrence, *The Practice of the Presence of God* (New Kensington, PA: Whitaker House, 1982), 17.

173. Lawrence, *Practice of the Presence*, 11.

174. Mendy Kaminker, "The Showbread: The How and Why of the Temple Offering," trans. Esther Rabi, Chabad.org, https://www.chabad.org/library/article_cdo/ aid/2974301/jewish/The-Showbread-The-How-and-Why-of-the-Temple-Bread-Offering.htm.

175. R. C. Sproul, *The Prayer of the Lord* (Sanford, FL: Ligonier Ministries, 2009), 71–72.

176. Deuteronomy 6:4.

177. Isaiah 35:1–2 NLT

wine

178. Ann Voskamp, *One Thousand Gifts: A Dare to Live Fully Right Where You Are*, 10th anniversary edition (Nashville, TN: Thomas Nelson, 2021), 9.

179. Elisabeth Elliot, *These Strange Ashes* (Grand Rapids, MI: Revell, 2023), https://books.google.com/ books?id=drjuEAAAQBAJ&pg=PT130&lpg=PT130&dq=Elisabeth+Elliot+A+ story+is+told+of+Jesus+and+His+disciples+walking+one+day+along+a+ stony+road.

180. Lawrence, *Practice of the Presence*, 18.

181. Dr. and Mrs. Howard Taylor, *The Spiritual Secret of Hudson Taylor* (New Kensington, PA: Whitaker House, 2003), 199.

182. Dr. and Mrs. Howard Taylor, *Hudson Taylor's Spiritual Secret* (Chicago: Moody Press, 1955), 202.

183. Taylor, *Spiritual Secret*, 161–162.

mangoes

184. Sherwood E. Wirt, *Jesus, Man of Joy* (Eugene, OR: Harvest House Publishers, 1999), 89.

185. Luke 13:34.

186. Hannah Whitall Smith, *The Christian's Secret of a Happy Life* (Uhrichsville, OH: Barbour Publishing, 2010), 47–48.

187. John of the Cross, *The Collected Works of St. John of the Cross*, trans. Kieran Kavanaugh and Otilio Rodríguez (ICS Publications, 1991), 97, https://www.goodreads.com/work/quotes/659664-obras-de-san-juan-de-la-cruz.

188. Mary A. Lathbury, "Break Thou the Bread of Life," 1877, https://hymnary.org/text/break_thou_the_bread_of_life.

189. Deuteronomy 6:7 AMPC.

190. Malachi 4:2 NRSVUE.

fish

191. Mahatma Gandhi, in *Young India*, 1931, https://quoteinvestigator.com/2020/01/29/hungry/.

192. Stewart Edward White, in *Pilgrim at Tinker Creek* by Annie Dillard (New York: Harper Perennial Modern Classics, 2013), 20.

193. See 1 Kings 19:1–18.

194. Robin Nixon Pompa, "Scientists Say We Can See Sound," Live Science, August 18, 2008, https://www.livescience.com/5045-scientists-sound.html.

195. Pompa, "Scientists Say We Can See Sound."

196. John 10:27 NKJV.

197. dmunger, "Tasting Words: A Study of One of the Rarest Forms of Synesthesia," ScienceBlogs, December 4, 2008, https://scienceblogs.com/cognitivedaily/2008/12/04/tasting-words-a-study-of-one-o.

198. John-Paul Clark, "Man with Rare Condition Who Can Taste and Smell Words Describes What Christmas Feels Like," Daily Record, December 10, 2022, https://www.dailyrecord.co.uk/news/uk-world-news/man-taste-smell-words-christmas-28700707.

199. Roberts Liardon and Olly Goldenberg, *God's Generals for Kids: William Seymour* (Newberry, FL: Bridge Logos, 2014), 61.

200. Acts 10:41 NLT.

201. Isaiah 52:7.

oil

202. Mother Teresa, A-Z Quotes, https://www.azquotes.com/quote/590401.

203. Chambers, *My Utmost for His Highest*, May 8.

204. Isaiah 43:1–2.

205. Anne Lamott, *Bird by Bird* (New York: Anchor Books, 1995), 13.

206. Jack Latimer, "The Legend of the Fig Tree Tomb," Our Watford History, February 26, 2014, https://www.ourwatfordhistory.org.uk/content/our-history/stmarys/the-legend-of-fig-tree-tomb; Rosemary Woodland, "The Famous Churchyard Fig Tree," This Is Local London, April 25, 2001, https://www.thisislocallondon.co.uk/news/140840.famous-churchyard-fig-tree/.

207. See, for example, Matthew 21:18–22.

208. Doherty, *Apostolic Farming*, 40.

209. Dutch Sheets, *The River of God* (Ventura, CA: Renew Books, 1998), 52.

210. Sheets, *River of God*, 53.

211. Sheets, 54.

212. See Isaiah 4:2.

213. Isaiah 32:2.

214. See Mark 8:22–25.

215. Taylor, *Hudson Taylor's Spiritual Secret*, 91–94.

216. See "The Asbury Outpouring," Asbury University, https://www.asbury.edu/outpouring/.

217. See Haggai 2:9.

218. Joel 2:24.

219. Amos 9:13.

220. Psalm 23:5 KJV.

benedicion

221. Calvin Miller, *The Words of Christ: An Everyday Journey with Jesus*, in "Words of Christ Quotes," Goodreads, https://www.goodreads.com/work/quotes/45688921-the-words-of-christ-an-everyday-journey-with-jesus.

222. Dinesen, *Babette's Feast*, 34.

223. Isaiah 53:7.

224. Psalm 33:6.

PART FOUR: KOINONIA

table

225. Shauna Niequist, *Bread and Wine: A Love Letter to Life Around the Table with Recipes* (Grand Rapids, MI: Zondervan, 2020), 226.

226. Emma Muscat, "Hidden In Plain Sight: The Fascinating Huguenot Practice Of Bible Concealment," News, Huguenot Museum, https://huguenotmuseum.org/about/news/hidden-in-plain-sight-the-fascinating-huguenot-practice-of-bible-concealment/.

227. John 6:51.

228. Romans 7:24–25.

229. Dorothy Day, *The Long Loneliness: The Autobiography of the Legendary Social Activist* (San Francisco: HarperCollins, 2009), 285.

230. Revelation 22:17.

About the Author

Photo courtesy The Lulu Tree Foundation, 2023

Emily T. Wierenga lives in northern Alberta, Canada, with her husband, Trenton, and their three children. She is passionate about the global church and advocating for the poor. An award-winning journalist, Emily is a columnist for the *Christian Courier* and a blogger, as well as a commissioned artist. Her writings have appeared in various print and online publications, including Christianity Today, Desiring God, the Gospel Coalition, and Focus on the Family Canada. She is also the author of several other books, including her previous two memoirs, *Atlas Girl: Finding Home in the Last Place I Thought to Look* and *Making It Home: Finding My Way to Peace, Identity, and Purpose,* the self-help resources *Chasing Silhouettes: How to Help a Loved One Battling an Eating Disorder* and *Mom in the Mirror: Body Image, Beauty and Life After Pregnancy* (with Dena Cabrera), and the novel *A Promise in Pieces* (Quilts of Love Series). She has been interviewed numerous times on *100 Huntley Street* and *My New Day* and has appeared on other programs and podcasts. Emily speaks regularly about her journey with anorexia nervosa and how she found healing through God's love. In 2014, she founded The Lulu Tree Foundation, where she currently serves as president.

Emily loves to kiss her husband of twenty years, hug her kids, snowboard, paint on canvas, read beautiful books, worship on her guitar, write words, "do church" at a local mental health drop-in center, and travel. Her favorite places are the poorest places. That's where she really sings.

Connect with Emily at www.emilytwierenga.com.

About The Lulu Tree Foundation

The Lulu Tree Foundation is a 501(c)(3) organization dedicated to preventing tomorrow's orphans by equipping today's families through the local church—with the greater mission of becoming one family in Christ. It currently operates in villages across West and East Africa, South Asia, and South America. For more information, visit www.thelulutree.com.

All proceeds from *God Who Became Bread* will benefit The Lulu Tree Foundation.